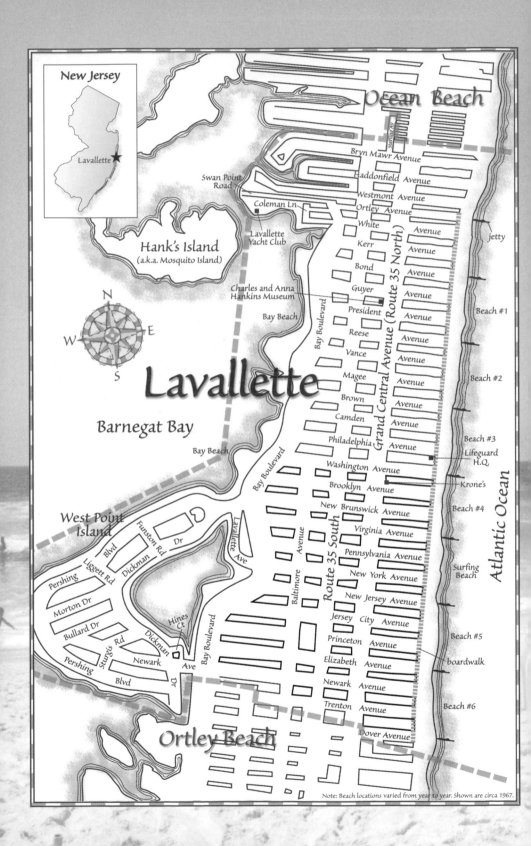

Note: Beach locations varied from year to year. Shown are circa 1967.

ALL SUMMER LONG

Tales and Lore of Lifeguarding on the Atlantic

GORDON HESSE

Jersey Shore Publications • Bay Head, New Jersey

Other titles from Jersey Shore Publications:
To The Shore Once More
To The Shore Once More, Volume II
A Gull's Story
Dick LaBonté, Paintings of the Jersey Shore and More
Ceramic Tile In 20th Century America
Spring Lake, Revisited

Magazines and Guide Books:
Jersey Shore Home & Garden
Jersey Shore Vacation Magazine
Jersey Shore Vacation Map
Jersey Shore Magazine & Guide

Jersey Shore Publications
Editor and Publisher: George C. Valente
P.O. Box 176, Bay Head, New Jersey 08742-0176
Telephone: 732-892-1276 • Fax: 732-892-3365
For Book Orders and Magazine Subscriptions, Toll Free: (888) 22-SHORE
www.jerseyshorevacation.com

▲ ▲ ▲

Front cover dust jacket photograph by John Ducsai
Back cover dust jacket photograph by Dick Meseroll
Wave illustration by Darren Hickman and Gordon Hesse

Title page photograph: Author Gordon Hesse, on the beach, early-1970s.

The typeface used on the cover is Goudy Bold.
The typeface used for the text is Times Roman.
The typefaces used for the chapter titles and subheads are Frutiger Light and Times Italic.
The paper is Maple Tradebook Natural Antique.

Printed and bound in the United States of America.

First Edition, April 2005

ISBN 0-9632906-7-3

Library of Congress Cataloging-in-Publication Data

Hesse, Gordon.
  All summer long : tales and lore of lifeguarding on the Atlantic / by Gordon Hesse.-- 1st ed.
     p. cm.
  ISBN 0-9632906-7-3 (hardcover with dustjacket : alk. paper)
  1. Lifesaving--New Jersey--Atlantic Coast--Anecdotes. 2. Lifeguards--New Jersey--Atlantic Coast--
Anecdotes. I. Title.
  GV838.4.N45H47 2005
  797'.028'9--dc22
                                    2005000085

This book is dedicated to Andrew Thomas Baran.
We began life together, just a few hours apart.
He was my Gemini twin, classmate,
surfboat rowing mate, bench partner, fellow deckhand,
colleague, raconteur extraordinaire,
and lifelong friend to many.

—G.H.

ALL SUMMER LONG

The 1952 Lavallette Beach Patrol. From left to right: First Row: Kenny Killian, Ray Williams, John Marra - Captain, Charlie Keller, and Dan Florko; **Second Row:** John Frayman, Rick Nolan, Ronald Marra, Jack Hart, Joe Fisher, and Gus Eppinger; **Third Row:** [first name unknown] Hart, George "Chippy" Mauro, and Bud Birch. The following two years, in '53 and '54, Ronald Marra, John's brother, served as Captain.

C O N T E N T S

...

Rudy Krone
('32-mid-'40s;
Captain)

Gordon "Mike"
Howes
('39-'41, '46-'54)

John Marra
('46-'53;
Captain '52-'53)

Dick Hoffman
('50-2000;
Captain '66-'80)

Sam Hammer
('62-'68)

Gordon Hesse
('65-'73, '75)

Andy Baran
('65-'70)

Mickey Howes
('67-'76)

Jim Cresbaugh
('67-present;
Captain '81-
present)

Jack Caucino
('77-present)

The Voices

The following are brief and highly subjective descriptions of some of the people quoted and mentioned in this book.

In a few cases, when an individual could not be located or contacted, limited third party information was gathered, and the person's actual name was not used.

In three cases, characters were created that are composites of various people. This was done at the request of individuals who wanted to remain annonymous in the events described and by the author to protect the innocent.

The years shown are the years they patrolled the beach.

Quoted in the text:

Andy B. - Andy Baran ('65-'70)

Dark-haired and blue-eyed, with an observant mind and the ability to mimic people's speech patterns, he prided himself on developing surfboat skills and became a top-notch lifeguard, participating in one of the largest known rescues in Lavallette.

Archie M. - Archie Mrozek ('58-'64)

Archie and his brother, Bob, both guarded in Lavallette.

Bob G. - Bob Ginglen ('63-'67, '69)

A quiet, soft-spoken person who never seemed to speak ill of anyone. His brother, Dick, was captain of the guards before Bob became a Lavallette Beach Patrol lieutenant.

Bobbi A. - Barbara "Bobbi" Alesso DeMuro ('65-'69)

One of the earliest female lifeguards at Lavallette, many were smitten by her smile and playful manner. Both she and her brother, Jimmy A., guarded in Lavallette at the same time.

Butch S. - Butch Spicoli (a composite character) (mid-'60s)

Butch had a high barrel chest and disproportionally long, skinny legs. He drank beer like it was water and was the prime mover for many parties. It seemed that whatever group he was with, laughter emanated.

Charlie B. - Charles Badeau ('65, '67-'71)

He had a short, stocky build, wore thick glasses, and managed to look all day long like he had just gotten out of bed.

Dave M. - Dave McConnell (late '60s, '74)

A fun-loving guard, he was a competitive swimmer and worked at the neighboring beaches in Seaside Park and the Surf Club in Ortley Beach.

Dick H. - Dick Hoffman ('50-2000; Captain '66-'80)

He guarded for nearly fifteen years before he was made captain of the Lavallette Beach Patrol. His U.S. Navy-developed skills were an asset in mending the ropes that were used to mark off bathing areas and to tether buoys.

Edwardo B. – Edwardo Black ('69-'70)

He went from working on the beach clean-up crew to lifeguarding when there was a shortage toward the end of the season. He drove a Corvette, and his family's bayfront home was the scene of several classic Viking parties.

Gordon H. - Gordon Hesse ('65-'73, '75)

Your author, and a Hankins surfboat devotee, he guarded in Lavallette, at the Surf Club in Ortley Beach, and at the Ponte Vedra Club in Florida. The son of the borough clerk, he became more detached from the younger guards during his later years of guarding.

Hobie - Cedric Huff (a composite character) ('65-'74)

Hobie was a laid-back, pot-smoking surfer who had practically been raised in saltwater. He had strawberry blond hair and managed to stay tanned all year-round. He brought West Coast sensibilities to the Jersey Shore and would drop whatever he was doing when the waves were good to kick out on his board.

Jack C. - Jack Caucino ('77-present)

From a family of highly competitive guards, he won numerous tournament events and became an assistant to the captain of the Lavallette Beach Patrol.

Jim C. - Jim Cresbaugh ('67-present; Captain '81-present)

A college quarterback, he brought competitive standards to the beach patrol when he became captain of the guards and beach manager.

Jim Sim - Jim Simms ('63-'77)

Recruited to lifeguarding by his football coach, Jim began patrolling the beaches at age sixteen and became well known for his ability to splice line. He worked on the beaches in Long Branch, New Jersey most of his career.

Jimmy A. - Jim Alesso ('66-'67)

Opinionated and playful, he and his sister, Bobbi A., guarded during the same period.

Joe S. - Joe Silvestri ('68-'76, '90s, '00s)

Short and built like a fireplug, he was one of the most conscientious and accommodating guards on the squad.

John M. - John Marra ('46-'53; Captain '52-'53)

A star sports competitor in his youth, he became a guard during a lifeguard strike and eventually captain of the guards. Uninformed guards soon learned he could swim out far beyond the normal bathing areas and would pay no heed to whistles instructing to the contrary.

John V. - John Van Dorpe ('66-'70)

After a short stint as a guard, he became a beach policeman. Often during rescues, he provided valuable support to the guards.

Jon S. - Jon Slayback ('66-'74)

For a time, he rode a Triumph motorcycle; he came to lifeguarding after working on the beach clean-up crews.

Kenny A. - Kenny Andersch (surfer) ('60s-'90s)

A massive surfer from Ortley, the town neighboring Lavallette to the south, "Paddlefoot" became known to the beach patrol through his friendship with the Howes family. Ken was well-acquainted with water conditions and hazards.

Kenny J. - Ken Jones ('67-'69)

Mellow and with a gentle southern charm, he swam competitively at Clemson University in South Carolina.

Michelle P. - Michelle Pierce ('77-'80, '83-'84)

One of the first female ocean lifeguards in Lavallette, she was a strong competitor in lifeguard tournaments.

Mickey H. - Mickey Howes ('67-'76)

The son and brother of lifeguards, he was one of the "surfer" guards who learned to swim almost before he could walk.

Mike H. - Gordon "Mike" Howes ('39-'41, '46-'54)

The father of Mickey and Colleen who also lifeguarded. As a youth, and during World War II, he visited beaches around the world and eventually became a leading East Coast figure in surfing.

Patricia D. - Pat Dughi ('67-'69)

A diminutive female guard, she worked the Barnegat Bay beaches where the work was more akin to babysitting than guarding.

Paul T. - Paul Tilton ('66-'73)

A competitive swimmer in high school, he worked at Lavallette and several other beaches.

Randy S. - Randy Smith (a composite character) ('60s)

Randy was strikingly good looking, had a bright intellect, quick wit, and a confident swagger. He seemed to have two distinct sides: some times he provoked confrontations and bordered on being a bully; other times he could show remarkable insight and sensitivity.

Ray B. - Ray Birchler ('55-'60)

The son of a borough councilman, his easy manner made him accessible and popular with the kids on the beach. He was known for his practical jokes.

Rudy K. - Rudy Krone ('32-mid-'40s; Captain)

One of the old guards, he was well-known by almost everyone in Lavallette. He was the proprietor of Krone's, a local tavern and restaurant. He served as lifeguard captain; both of his sons also lifeguarded.

Russell F. - Russell Frazier ('50-'51)

With a tall frame and ruddy complexion, he was a "hail fellow, well met." Although he was only a lifeguard for two summers, Russ was well-known to the beach crews who followed him. He became a strong supporter of the beach patrol and considered lifeguarding to be one of the best jobs he ever had.

Sam H. - Sam Hammer ('62-'68)

The towheaded son of a physician, he was disarming and sociable with all, with an abundant, self-deprecating humor. He taught preventative lifeguarding, and when not on the beach, loved to cook and have parties.

Sharon M. - Sharon Mill (beachgoer) ('60s-present)

Sharon and her twin sister became well-known to the beach patrol from their acquaintances with several of the guards.

Tom A. - Tom Azzolini ('63-'70)

Quick-witted and friendly, he was the oldest of a family of lifeguards. A proud native of Hoboken, New Jersey, he was always entertaining to spend a day with on the stand, spouting theories on all manners of society.

Mentioned in the text:

Bill Kemble ('50s-'70s)

Bill was the familiar dispatcher at the lifeguard headquarters. He wore khaki shirts and pants, smoked fat cigar stubs, and his lunch often included brandy-soaked blueberries.

Charles Hankins

Charles Hankins & Sons built surfboats that were highly prized among lifeguards for their ability to cut through large waves when launched from the beach.

"Duke" - Frank DeLuca ('60s)

His distinctive round nose coated in zinc oxide added to the colorful, humorous lifeguard he became. He had a soft southern drawl, reportedly returned to Florida, and has not been heard from since.

Eddie V. - Ed Verna (early '60s)

Shorter than many of the guards, he moonlighted part of his guarding career, working when he could get leave from his military obligations at a nearby installation.

"Jake" J. - Tom Jacobsen ('65-'69)

Tall and from Scandanavian stock, he towered over the entire squad. He had a mean streak that no one wanted to evoke.

John T. - John Tawgin ('64-'65, '69)

Rakishly good-looking and urbane, he was part of an inner clique of guards who had grown up together on the beach. Part of his guarding career consisted of working on weekends when a larger patrol was needed.

Pete L. - Pete Locascio ('64-'74)

Having a heavy-set build, with dark wavy hair and strong Italian features, Pete exuded confidence and delighted in taunting pompous figures of authority.

Roger K. - Roger Krone ('64-'68)

Good-looking, brilliant, and socially adept, he always seemed to be dating some of the most beautiful women on the beach. His wit was sharp, and he was close friends with several of the guards.

"The Whale" – Dominic Arena (late '50s)

One of the legends of Lavallette Beach Patrol lore, "The Whale" was extremely powerful and popular with the kids on the beach. He started out as a beach cop and later became a lifeguard.

The 1965 Lavallette Beach Patrol a.k.a. "The Vikings." This photo was taken at the end of the season. Many of the guards had returned to college and are not shown. A mobile home trailer was used as the lifeguard office that year. **From left to right: First Row:** Dick Hoffman, Fosdick Ayer, Bob Ginglen, Frank DeLuca, Roger Krone, Dick Ginglen - Captain, and Sam Hammer; **Second Row:** Gene Ventimiglia, Mel Russen, Jay Gaskill, Tom Jacobsen (obscured), Les Smith, [name unknown], and Ron Mopsic. In the trailer doorway, just barely visible, is Bill Kemble.

Preface
Bonds On The Beach

All ocean beaches are the same. From one sunrise to the next, with the rotations of the moon exerting invisible powers, the tide rises twice and lowers. Cosmic impulses that began before time imaginable form sea vibrations that combine with the wind to ripple across thousands of miles of ocean, ending on the shore as a crashing wave or a murmured lap.

All beaches are different. The currents, the temperatures, the prevailing winds, and the nature of the bottom all create a brew of variables. The coast may be lined with rock, marsh, or sand—finely-ground by the ages and heaped in bluffs, topped with tall stalks of wild grass, beach plum, sumac, and bayberry. The beach may have high sandbars that produce long, building waves that crack as they fold. Or the water may be deep with sharp shorebreak drops where the waves snap suddenly, explode, and shoot out, sweeping the beach with new sand and the broken hulls of sea life from long ago, before retreating to begin anew.

For nine summers and part of a spring (from '65 to '73 and in '75), I was a professional beach watcher—a lifeguard. This was much better than in my earlier years when I was an amateur beach observer and did not get paid anything for the spying delights of the beach. Whereas before I had been a nosey gawker, now in my vigilant, yet professional role, I had a license to stare and watch, to scrutinize and analyze everything. Only the horizon was my boundary.

It always struck me as ironic that I was paid to sit in a high chair and baby-sit adults, teens, and families. It was great work most of the time, and ideal for one given to contemplation, observation, and analysis. On the majority of days, the water was calm and dangers rare. On those days, it offered visual Zen meditations amid the soft sounds of bathers communing with a mysterious part of their past, the light chimes of children at discovery, and the muted, easy tempo of the folding waves.

I have heard that the salt content of the human body matches that of the ocean. Perhaps there is a connection deeper than we know. The ocean beach provides a natural wonderland for children to frolic and a place to be lost in the elements of sun and breezes that sometimes seem to breathe.

Although there were times when I was alone, it was not often solitary work. I usually had a bench partner to provide better surveillance and act as an emergency complement.

Bench partners came with different experiences and in different sizes. You got to know each other well, for you would spend the greater part of each work day sitting on a stand and observing beach theater together. You worked side by side for weeks, sometimes even months. Personality and trust were critical elements for the wedding of work.

The veteran partner who broke you in helped to shape the kind of guard you became. You learned how to deal with the public, keys to spotting developing hazards, and even how to bite into a whistle as you blew for maximum volume, sharpness, and impact. Because in my day the veteran guards had been to college already, you also had help in learning how to drink beer and advance a relationship.

A good partner could do the job of watching for developing danger, react to it quickly and wisely, and return life to a safer balance. The most complementary partners could anticipate each other's actions in a tight spot. A really good bench partner could also give interesting commentary and analysis to the unfolding scene, or, at the very least, strike upon a vein of conversation that was of mutual interest. Invariably, most of the conversations seemed to dwell on the opposite gender, and sex, but discussion could delve into the arts, politics, religion, sports, and family. It could be both profane and profound. Over time, many of us—through shared experiences, both good and bad—forged a bond on the beach that will remain forever.

I found camaraderie among lifeguards that spanned generations and locales. It is not uncommon for guards from one decade or one beach patrol to share experiences—some universal among lifeguards and some distinctly unique—with those from another time and place, particularly among those who have shown themselves worthy of the brotherhood.

They have witnessed and participated in the primitive aspects of life held in the balance. They have had the opportunity to swing the odds towards life by pitting their wit, muscle, and grit against ageless natural elements. They have seen the face that is confronting immediate mortality and have won the confrontation.

Nearly all the partners I worked with were college educated; hence the conversations were often an education in themselves. Indeed, an oral tradition is as much a part of lifeguarding as were the tales of *Ulysses* or *Beowulf* before they were put down on paper.

It was while meeting with generations of lifeguard friends that I realized the rich oral tradition of these men and women, and the idea for this book, a compilation of beach culture and life that traces the evolution of lifeguarding on the Atlantic, took form.

I began to write down my own experiences from my ten years as an ocean lifeguard and to interview and tape the guards I had worked with as well as some of the earliest guards at the Jersey Shore; I interviewed and corresponded with nearly three dozen men and women with experiences spanning seven decades, from the '30s through the '90s.

These first-person accounts and recollections were transcribed and edited. A few words were changed and punctuation was added to clarify the idiosyncrasies of the spoken word; however, I chose to preserve the actual words and diction of the voices over editing them into "grammatically correct" sentences. Thus, the voice and character of the person comes through more clearly to the reader.

The different voices in this book offer insight into the heritage, training, hazing, groupies, triumphs, and tragedies of lifeguarding, as well as skills and observations that have been handed down from generation to generation. They also provide valuable safety tips and mark some of the significant changes in guarding, including the introduction and acceptance of women as ocean lifeguards.

This book is an attempt to record a part of the oral tradition and culture of lifeguarding, to gather reflections upon experiences, and to preserve some of these voices of the beach. At times it may be as ethereal as the joyous squeals of small children splashing in the foam of the low tide, or as obvious as a shorebreak. These accounts are little more than tiny tiles in a mosaic; but when taken as a whole, they offer each reader a different picture colored by their own experiences. Although most of these recollections are snapshots in time from a small coastal town on the Jersey Shore, ocean lifeguards from practically anywhere or anytime may find something of their own experiences in this microcosm.

This book is also an attempt to pass along part of the training and experience that isn't written in the lifesaving manuals—but is instead normally passed along from one guard to another. It is my hope to teach a few lessons hard learned and record the deeds of these small but mighty men and women who guarded our beaches. It is my hope that it can offer the shared wisdom of many experiences and recapture what it is like to be a catcher in the rye.

—Gordon Hesse
December 31, 2004

The 1966 Lavallette Beach Patrol. This photograph includes many of the core voices in this book. **From left to right: Kneeling:** Dick Hoffman - Lieutenant, and Dick Ginglen - Captain; **First Row:** [name unknown], Rich MacAniff, Mary Barnett, Barbara "Bobbi" Alesso DeMuro, Pat Grosko, Joe McBride, David Ratcliffe, and Andy Baran; **Second Row:** John Van Dorpe, Les Smith, Paul Tilton, Roger Krone, Sam Hammer, [name unknown], Ron Mopsick, and Steve Anteau; **Back Row:** Marty Gaukstern, Steve Gaskill, Tom "Jake" Jacobsen, and Bob Ginglen.

The 1973 Lavallette Beach Patrol. From left to right: First Row, kneeling: Rich Radcliffe, Ray Rowland, Charlie Furey, Jim Cresbaugh - Lieutenant, Ken Chapin, Steve Graves, Dick Hoffman - Captain, Bob O'Brien, Joe Matusewicz, and Steve DuFrense; **Second Row:** Roy Fischer, Wendy Bromly, Roz Caruso, Mickey Howes, Larry Barney(?), Chia Sabarese, and Lori Hoffman; **Third Row:** George Thompson, John Godfrey, Bill O'Brien, Greg Ciggelakis, Jay Pumphrey, Jon Slayback, Doug Murray, Carl Caucino, and Bob Konowicz; **Fourth Row:** Jim Caruso, Rick Keppler, Bob "Whale" Davis, Carl D'Alessandro, Tom Rack, Tom Arden, Parker Snare, and Paul Lenzo. Please note: The names of the people in this photo were not recorded at the time it was taken. Identities were presumed through a variety of sources.

Introduction
Now And Then

*I*t was the organizational meeting of the 1997 Lavallette Beach Patrol at the Jersey Shore. As this season's lifeguards (veterans and rookies alike) came in with their three-page applications, passports to attest to their nationality, and lots of paper work, I couldn't help but think about how things had changed since I had last guarded in 1976.

The guards were younger. Many of them were not even old enough to shave. When I guarded, you had to be at least eighteen years old. Back then, three or four guys could split the rent on a shack and still pocket some money. Now, it is so hard to find kids of college age that can afford to live at the beach and guard that they have lowered the age limit to sixteen. Most of the kids now come from out of town; some don't seem too familiar with the ocean.

Now there were more women guards. And they were working on the ocean.

In my days on the Beach Patrol, the novelty of women lifeguards was beginning to wear off, but they were only used to guard on the tame, tepid waters of Barnegat Bay. They went years without rescues and were little more than glorified babysitters. Before women began guarding, guarding on the bay was considered the "penalty box"—a sentence for lifeguards who had committed indiscretions.

During the Beach Patrol meeting, I learned that the guards followed standards for national certification.

There were other changes: hepatitis shots, rubber gloves packed in the first aid kits, guard training from VCR tapes, and each beach had portable radios. They had squads and unit competitions.

There was new equipment. Along with the same gear we had, they had a fully-equipped truck, two-way radios, and rescue kayaks and backboards for supporting injury victims.

And the operations had changed. Now there were two more ocean beaches. Each beach had three guards instead of the two when I began guarding in the mid-'60s. It seemed like saturation to me, but I guess it made sense: if you have less experience, you compensate with more personnel.

Because of the increase in duties, the captain of the guards is now called the beach manager. Instead of just being in charge of the lifeguards, he also administers to beach clean-up crews, beach badge checkers, and swimming instructors.

Perhaps the most striking difference was the structure and discipline that the beach manager had established in his nearly twenty years as beach captain. Now a high school administrator, he was a rookie guard my third year of guarding. Although the admonitions were similar to my day, back then, like the cocky stars on the team in the movie *Rollerball*, we scoffed and did our best to circumvent them.

The list of "Do's" sounded similar, even familiar at first:

Get on "shack time"—late three times and you are out.
Drive safely.
Wear belt and whistle at all times.
Call-in when you set up.

Remember you represent the borough.

Shave (along with the age-old threat: *"We have rusty razors in the back, and we'll show you how to shave if you've forgotten."*)

Hair is to be worn short.

Women must tie their hair back if it is long.

No profanity—don't lower yourselves to people who are using it.

Avoid heated arguments.

No meeting guards from the adjacent beach at the jetties.

Use the whistle as a last resort.

When making reports, make statements of facts.

Read the instructions on how to replace toilet paper in the lifeguard shack restroom.

So far, I recalled getting almost the same instructions—and someone violating at least one of them nearly every day.

Then came some surprises when they got to the "Don'ts":

Don't wear anything other than issued equipment.

No reading or playing games on the bench—chess, tic-tac-toe, etc.

Don't leave the stand without a torpedo buoy.

Don't wear mirror sunglasses—you want to make eye contact.

Then the regimentation:

Sign in before 9:00 a.m.

Training exercises are daily from 9:00 - 9:40 a.m.

Gee, after the third week of the season, we only had workouts when too many of the guards were hungover.

The beach is open from 10:00 a.m. - 5:00 p.m.

Hmmm, we used to work until 6:00 p.m.

Beach badge checkers are stationed on the beach from 10:00 - 3:00 p.m.

Even the after-work activities seemed structured:

Lifeguarding tournaments.

Barbecues.

Trips to minor league baseball games.

Shuffleboard.

Shuffleboard? Are you kidding me?

Trips to the movies.

Miniature golf.

Miniature golf? In the back of my mind, I could hear the ghosts of the veterans I guarded with elbowing each other and howling in derision.

Then the beach manager mentioned some innovations:

Junior Lifeguard training three afternoons each week.

Fundraising.

Well, we did that. We'd throw a dance and raffle a "basket of cheer" to make a couple hundred and spend it on a banquet at the end of the summer. One year we even helped one of the guards who busted his leg in a softball game and had no income. But these guys had gotten into marketing.

They had a local Boosters Club buy Van Dyne Surfboats and surfboards for competitions. They sold imprinted tee shirts, water bottles, tank tops, and hats. They even had a soda machine with the proceeds going to the Boosters Club.

Then the beach manager talked about the competitions and fitness:

Inner squad tournaments—usually on Sundays.

Women's tournament. County tournament.

Workouts for tournament contestants from 7:30 - 8:30 a.m.

They were told to bring running shoes for workouts on inclement days.

I would become aware, later during the season, of how polished these new guards were. They had established a fine reputation for winning tournaments, particularly over the last two decades, and for performing their jobs well as public servants.

I thought back to the guys I guarded with. What a motley crew we must have been. I thought about several who were either overweight or wore thick glasses; others smoked cigarettes on the stand or drank liquor on rainy days (and even on days when the sun was out). One of the captains of the guards was not above tipping one with the crew.

In the late 1960s, when alcohol lost some of its prestige, some guys actually drank electric Kool Aid—LSD-laced punch—when it seemed like the rain was going to last all day. Others just toked on a roach during a "head" break. I recall bench partners hunching behind sunglasses and taking turns sleeping on the stands.

But amazingly, they always did their primary job: they did not let anyone drown! They provided first aid, and they helped people avoid distressing situations.

You could say their secondary job was to have fun in one of the best jobs in the world.

The 1939 Lavallette Beach Patrol - "Atlantic Coast Lifeguard Champions."
From left to right: Rudy Krone, Harry Bloom, Elmer Brackman, and Al Krone.
These lifeguards competed against various East Coast lifeguards from New York City
to Miami to win highest honors.

Spring
Beginnings

Monmouth and Ocean counties comprise the central Jersey coastal region. To the north, Monmouth County consists of farmland and rivers that give way to harbors and inlets. Beaches in Monmouth tend to have more jetties and boardwalks than the land to the south, which was developed later. Long Branch, Asbury Park, Belmar, Spring Lake, and Manasquan are some of its better-known beach communities. Originally, they had catered to city dwellers trying to escape the heat and take in the offshore breezes.

Further south down the coast is the Manasquan Inlet, the natural boundary between the two counties. Here the land becomes a peninsula with a large, mile-wide bay that extends south for about twenty miles before reaching Barnegat Inlet and Barnegat Lighthouse. The major coastal communities in Ocean County are Point Pleasant Beach, Bay Head, Mantoloking, Ocean Beach, Lavallette, Ortley Beach, Seaside Heights, Seaside Park, and Island Beach State Park, a ten-mile stretch of land left almost in the same pristine condition as when Henry

Hudson sailed the region, with the exception of one main road and several bathing houses and parking areas. The next coastal landmass, known as Long Beach Island, consists of several communities including Beach Haven and Ship Bottom. South of Ocean County are the popular resort towns of Atlantic City, Ocean City, Wildwood, and Cape May.

Each of the beaches along this stretch of coast has its own character. In northern Ocean County, the beaches drop off with almost no sandbar. Further south, the shifting sandbars tend to be more pronounced. To the very south of the state, the beach tends to slowly recede further below the surface. The beach sand there tends to be finer and to compact harder.

♦ ♦ ♦

The First New Jersey Lifeguards

From "The History of Lavallette, 1887-1997," second edition:

The Beginning Of The Lavallette Beach Patrol

The Patrol got its start in 1926, so the story goes, when Mayor Enoch T. Van Camp watched three residents risk their lives to bring ashore a bather who had overestimated his swimming ability. "Nucky" waited long enough to order the bather's arrest for endangering his rescuers, then declared, "We gotta have a boat." Accordingly, a skiff was ordered from Charles M. Hankins, and when it was delivered, Ralph Helmuth was appointed to man it.

Fort Colie Brice [sic] walked the beach as the first paid lifeguard in the summer of 1926. The beach then only ran the length of the boardwalk between New Brunswick and Ortley Avenues; the protected part was determined by the configuration of the shoreline in any particular year.

...There was little need for formal training or testing in the early days. Growing up in Lavallette, the guards were powerful if not polished swimmers. They were accustomed to handling rowboats far less

seaworthy than the patrol's skiffs and were wise in the ways of the
waves and currents.

Early Years Of Lifeguarding In Lavallette

RUDY K. ('32-mid-'40s; Captain) - Everybody in Lavallette was
from Philadelphia back then. People came on the Sunday train excur-
sions. The trains came from Philadelphia and the University of
Pennsylvania. People wore ties and garters and went to the Roan Club.
North Jersey wasn't even big then.

I started lifeguarding in 1932. Then there were only two guards.
One was at President Avenue and the other was south of Vance. Before
me was Colie Brice and Randolph Jacobsen (Old Jake). Then there was
Tony Ryan, Dave Bendy, Old Jake, and myself. I guarded for about
twenty-five years, even after Ralph (my son) was born. I also guarded
in Sea Bay Park for a few years.

Guarding in those days was bare bones. We had Hankins boats,
stands, and torpedo buoys. The buoys were made of tin by Gabriel in
Seaside Heights. There was always a station at President Avenue.

A Drowning In The '30s

RUDY K. - It was around 1934 when we had a bad northeastern.
Elmer B. and I were guards together on Vance or Reese Avenues. I
think we were the only ones on. People came hollering for us. They
told us there were people out there off of Ortley Avenue—about six
blocks away. We put the boat in the water, rowed up to Ortley Avenue,
and we got to two or three people. Elmer pulled them into the boat—
he was built like a house. We took them onto the beach and then found
out there was another person we didn't know about. We launched the
boat again, and a big comber came, and we got swamped. We knew
there was no chance of finding him, but we went out for the benefit of
the family. He was a nice young man. He washed up either later that
day or the next day.

The Atlantic Coast Lifeguard Championships of '38, '39, and '40

RUDY K. - When we started the lifeguard championships in 1938, we didn't know what the hell we were doing. But the next year we had four events:

1. a 300 - 500 yard rope pull (swimming out to a standard on a buoy)
2. a swim race out to the buoy and back
3. a short boat race (out and back)
4. a one-mile or more race out to the outer most pound poles

I did the swimming. Wildwood, Beach Haven, Miami, Florida, the New York City Parks (Rye Beach and Coney Island), Belmar, and Asbury Park all competed. We won in 1939 and got a big trophy. Our boat was specially built by Hankins. It was made of lightweight pine and cedar, and we kept it dry for several weeks. It was the same shape as the regular surfboats, but it was so light that two men could pick it up. Then we Simonized it for several days so it would slide easier. We sure did Hankins a lot of good.

In 1940, we would have won except Elmer Brackman broke an oar going out, so we were pretty much out of that race. Instead of using oak oars, we were using lightweight pine—that's probably why it broke. We had won the rope pull—I came in first. Atlantic City squawked and got my brother and I disqualified because he had put a knee down, or I had carried him. But they were no better. For the line pull, their swimmer wore a jacket over his shoulders to conceal the coiled line which he had tied with "sugar" string (light string used in grocery stores back then to tie up parcels). It was a damn good idea. The swimmer carried the coiled line close to him as he swam. When he got close to the buoy and the line was getting heavy with the current, he snapped the sugar string and uncoiled the line, making it easier for him to sprint to the end. We had our own tricks, though. We didn't use our regular line either; it was made of cotton. It wasn't that heavy, and it would float.

Ocean City showed up with a boat that was great in calm water. It was more like a scull. They held their competition on the back bay where the water was calm to give them an advantage.

After a while, the competition rules got more stringent.

Guarding Influences

MIKE H. ('39-'41, '46-'54) - Probably one of the persons most influential on my lifesaving career was Howard Roland. Howard was the captain of either the Asbury Park or Belmar lifeguard squads during the 1930s. He was probably one of the best watermen that ever lived in New Jersey. My cousin and I took a senior lifesaving course from him in the winter of 1935. The classes were held once a week in Asbury Park at night. Bob and I would have to hitchhike nearly twenty-five miles to attend the classes. Going up early in the night was not too bad, but coming home after class sometimes got really rough.

Howard was a really big guy and believed that you should be able to handle a struggling person when you were making a rescue. Every time we had to rescue him in the pool, he really fought hard, and it was a major effort to get him in. By the end of the night we were exhausted, and then we had to go outside in subfreezing temperatures and try to hitchhike back to Toms River. Sixty years ago, there were not so many people living in that part of New Jersey as there are now. There was a lot of empty land between Asbury Park and Toms River and not many cars late on a weeknight. Sometimes it would take us hours to get home. I remember one night, it was so cold, we had to go into a church to get warm for a while.

Another influential person was Commodore Longfellow. He was the founder of the Red Cross Lifesaving Program. I took a few courses from him when I first became involved with the Red Cross. Captain Skully of the Long Island Beach Patrol was also a major influence.

Guarding As A Family Tradition

ANDY B. ('65-'70) - Lifeguarding is a part of the Baran family tradition. My father started guarding at the Strand Beach in Seaside Heights in 1935 at age eighteen, at about the same time that his family was discovering the resort paradise at the Ocean County shore. For years, they had taken day trips to Cliffwood Beach, driving two hours each way from Elizabeth on the ancient roads of the time. When (through other family members) they discovered Lavallette, a tiny spit of brush-covered wilderness with rolling sand dunes bisected by the Route 35 dirt highway, they immediately fell in love with the area and made plans to make it their summer vacation spot, eventually building the bungalow in 1937 which would eventually become my home.

From Strand Beach, Dad became a Lavallette guard during the late 1930s, just before joining the Marines prior to the outbreak of war. After the war, while on R&R, Dad, along with Irv Humphrey, one of his war buddies, again worked as a Lavallette guard. The two of them built a shack on Hank's Island (a.k.a. Mosquito Island) in Barnegat Bay, just across from the Lavallette Yacht Club. They would row in every morning and row back home at night. It was during this time that he met and married a twenty-two-year-old war widow after a three-week courtship. I was always grateful for the chance meeting of this war veteran and this girl while she was wheeling her two-year old infant child on the boardwalk off Reese Avenue. The two of them carried on a long and happy life together, bearing up under good times, heartaches, and tragedy, separated only by death twenty-seven years later.

After leaving Lavallette to guard at a private beach two miles north of town, my father had the burden of breaking in his kid brother, an overgrown, sixteen-year-old man-child, my Uncle Richard. In this role, my father had to act as a disciplinarian, trying to monitor my uncle's sexual and alcoholic excesses, both on and off the beach.

One story that both of them would tell me, from their two totally different perspectives, was about a young lady who was looking for attention. The occasion occurred when Richard was rowing his skiff just outside the swimming area, and one of his young girlfriends swam out to him, boarded his boat, and after admonishing him for not paying proper attention to her, demanded what Richard termed "service." Richard, who was never one to be recalcitrant in such matters, immediately obliged. So on a sunny day, with a beach full of people, Richard was mounted by this Lolita while her unsuspecting parents sat on the beach not one hundred yards away. My father would get apoplectic whenever he told this story, squirming with anguish at the memory alone.

Richard became a Lavallette guard during the late '40s to early '50s. He was physically agile and athletic, earning the name "Cuda" for his incredible swimming ability. As with my father, he was also an accomplished boatsman.

The Early Days

MIKE H. - I was born in Toms River in 1920 and spent every summer on the beach at Ortley Beach until 1978. My father bought two hundred feet of beach in Ortley, just north of the Surf Club, in the early 1940s. I built six summer rental houses on that property in the 1950s and watched them wash out to sea in the Great March Storm of 1962. So, I guess I have seen over fifty years at the Jersey Shore. I lived at a house on the beach year-round from 1963 to 1978. During that time, I saw a lot of changes. When I was a kid, we could just cruise the beach in our beach buggies with no restrictions. Most of Ortley Beach and Lavallette consisted of sand dunes. We had to cross Barnegat Bay on two-lane wooden bridges.

I became involved with the Red Cross and lifesaving as a teenager in the 1930s. In 1937, I went to Atlantic City to see a demonstration of surfing by Duke Kahanamoku and Tom Blake on the famous "Blake Board." Based on what I saw, I went home and my father and I made what was probably the first surfboard in New Jersey, if not the east coast. Then three of my friends and I taught ourselves to surf. My friends and I started to surf regularly each summer after that. The summer of 1941, before we entered World War II, I made an 8-mm surf movie about surfing in New Jersey and using Blake Boards for rescue purposes. I have since converted that to a video to preserve it for my grandson and the future generations.

My cousin Bob and I were the first lifeguards in Ortley Beach when we started guarding in 1939. Our equipment consisted of a metal torpedo, beach blanket, umbrella, surf mat, and my surfboard. I had to watch from the Surf Club down to Vision Beach. The same area is probably covered by at least twelve guards with radios nowadays. After the war, when I was captain of the guards in Ortley, we staffed up to two benches on the north end of town and three benches on the south end on the weekends. On the weekdays, this was reduced to one on the north and two on the south so people could have a day off.

I always felt that a lifeguard's main responsibility was to keep people out of trouble, not make a lot of rescues. I felt that if a guard was always making rescues, he did not know the water and should be replaced. There are always exceptions and rough days where no matter what you did, someone would get into trouble, but on the whole, a good guard should be able to keep people out of trouble rather than rescuing them when they did get into trouble.

Surfboats—Not Just Another Rowboat

ANDY B. - Boats were an important tool in the early days of lifeguarding when the beaches were spread out and bathers had more freedom to wander from the shore, thus engendering long-distance rescues. The surfboats were indispensable. In this case, the good surfboat—the only surfboat—was the Hankins skiff. My father once told me that the original Hankins skiff, designed and built by the Hankins Brothers during the 1930s, was much longer and had a more streamlined sweep than later models. Dad compared the early skiff to the wooden rocker on the bottom of a rocking chair: a high bow and an even higher transom with gunnels so low that they almost seemed at times to touch the water. It was this design that enabled the boat to maneuver through the roughest surfs by "rocking" up and over the waves rather than plowing through them and swamping.

Dad had been on the famous group of guards in 1939 who hosted and won an invitational competition comprised of teams coming from as far away as Atlantic Highlands and Atlantic City, both nearly forty miles away to the north and south respectively. Also on the team were Rudy and Al Krone as well as El Brackman and Harry Bloom. My father swore that the main reason for the victory of the Lavallette boys was the existence of the Hankins surfboat and the incredible ability of Greek gods such as Brackman and Bloom to row and maneuver this magnificent craft.

Uncle Richard, in keeping with the tradition, was a skilled and strong boatsman. Both he and Dick Hoffman (who would become captain of the guards and whom I would guard with in later years) both recalled the time that the two of them, accompanied by Jim Frazier, took a Hankins boat out in the wake of an early '50s hurricane to "ride some waves." Such an undertaking would make a whaler's Nantucket Sleigh Ride look like a walk in the park.

To prime themselves for the job, the three of them split two six-packs of Ballantine Ale. Miraculously, they made it outside of the break, and with Richard at the tiller oar, took two large waves all the way into the beach. Frazier and Hoffman shifted their weight toward the stern once the wave was assured to keep the bow of the boat from "pearling" and thus avoiding disaster. However, on the third wave they weren't quick enough. The trajectory of the monster wave drove the bow deep into the water with the crew, oars and all, being catapulted into the hurricane surf. Somehow, the capsized boat was maneuvered to the beach safely, and the courageous and lucky trio beat a hasty retreat and survived to fight another day.

How I Became A Lifeguard At Age Fourteen

JOHN M. ('46-'53; Captain '52-'53) - In 1944, all the local guys that worked on the beach—the Barans, the Blooms, the Brackmans, Coley Brice—had gone on strike. They just refused to work. They were getting $.84 an hour, and they wanted $1.00 an hour. Rather than give in to their demands, the guy that was the captain, a nice little guy by the name of Roland P. Goddard, looked for replacements. He was a personal friend of the councilman that was in charge of the beach.

Anyway, he said to me, "Hey kid, wanna lifeguard?"

I knew how to swim, so I said sure, even though I was only fourteen.

He said, "Go sit on that stand and guard."

And that's how I got started working on the beach. I finished out the year, even though I didn't have any training. Afterward, I was a Boy Scout, so I took lifesaving for a merit badge.

After I worked for several years, when I was twenty-one and twenty-two, I became the captain of the guards. Back then we had sixteen lifeguards—seven beaches on the ocean and two on the bay.

Rubber Bathing Suit

MIKE H. - Just after World War II, they introduced skin-tight rubber bathing suits. They did not last very long since they were not especially comfortable and had other design problems. Once they started to tear, even a little, the rubber continued to split. One day a woman was standing at the edge when a large shorebreak hit her. It ripped the suit, and the whole thing split open like a torn rubber band. The suit shot away from her, and she was left standing stark naked at the water's edge.

The Big Assist

MIKE H. - The biggest rescue/assist I was ever involved with occurred in the summer of 1947 in the south part of Ortley Beach. It was one of those perfect, late August days. The water was warm and clear, and the surf was only about two feet. There was a massive sandbar a long ways out. In the morning, there was a really low tide so people only had to walk through waist-deep water to get out to it. Before long, there were several hundred people, including lots of little kids standing on the bar.

In a few hours, the southeast wind started to blow, and the tide began to come in really fast. All of a sudden, these people that were able to walk out to the bar through shallow water carrying their kids realized that they were standing on a sandbar a long way from shore with a lot of deep water between them and the beach—and the tide was coming in. Quite a few of them started panicking and yelling for help. Since there were only four of us to cover the entire south end of Ortley, there was no way we could help in all of them at the same time. We got all the teenage kids on the beach that had surf mats and organized a taxi service and taxied all the kids and weak swimmers back to the beach on the surf mats. The local kids got a really big kick out of helping the lifeguards bring the tourists to the beach.

Target Practice

MIKE H. - In 1948, when I was guarding the south end of Ortley Beach, we got a call from Seaside Heights about some sharks heading our way. We immediately got everyone out of the water, and a little while later, we saw a couple of sharks cruising north. They were in really close. You could actually see them swimming through the waves as they went by. One of our local policemen showed up and took a few shots at them with his service revolver. I doubt if he hit them, but everyone on the beach was cheering.

The Drift Of Longshore Currents

MIKE H. - A lot of guards knew how to spot a rip, but never had a good understanding of how the longshore current or drift could move someone from a safe area into a rip. The longshore currents usually ran from south to north because of the prevailing southeast wind; however, this was reversed when we had a northeast wind. These currents would pull people along the beach and right into a rip. On windy days, you had to constantly watch people and herd them away from the rips before they got in trouble. The average tourist had no idea what was happening or where the longshore current was taking them. On slow days, when I was first guarding, I used to take fish net floats and tie a sinker to them, then throw them into the water to see how the current would take them down the beach. This gave me the ability to really understand the currents.

Surf Show

ANDY B. - As a kid growing up, my biggest thrill during the summer was watching the lifeguards launch a Hankins skiff and somehow row it through rough surf. There was an almost magical quality to the sight of the oars madly digging into the water, the bow of the boat barely clearing a cresting wave, and the reverberating slap as the bottom of the boat slammed on the water surface. Even more exciting was watching the guards catch waves in the seventeen-foot craft. The teamwork and timing involved was a subject of fascination: two pairs of arms pulling maniacally at oars to get a five hundred pound boat up to speed to keep pace with a forming breaker. It called for pinpoint timing. As they simultaneously shipped oars, the guard in the rear seat dove to the stern to grab the tiller oar, digging it into the water to stabilize the boat, while the other guard dove first to the stern to keep the boat from pearling and then raced to the bow once the boat planed on an even keel.

My father was a lover of Hankins boats. Not only was he the owner of a Hankins surfboat, but he also had a twenty-five-foot lap strake shell. He outfitted it by himself, building on a cabin and dropping in a huge Chrysler engine. The boat cut through the most treacherous waters like a hot knife through butter and never faltered going through the Manasquan Inlet, even during a northeast wind.

Surfboats And Torpedo Buoys

JOHN M. - We used to do a lot of crazy things. I think boats today are used primarily for competition. In the 1940s and '50s, we almost always used the boats for rescues. Back then, we only had two things: the boat and a torpedo buoy with a rope. Today, they have about forty lifeguards with plenty of backup.

Back in my day, the worst thing that the guards did on duty was to go up to someone's house on the oceanfront and watch the beach from a house or a garage that was close to the ocean. I don't remember any-one drinking on the job then—they probably drank at night, though.

We'd do crazy things—like taking the lifeboats out in northeasters.

Big Sting Rays

MICKEY H. ('67-'76) - Stingrays were very rare in New Jersey. In the twenty-seven years I spent on the beach, I only saw them twice. The stingrays I'm talking about aren't the little ones the size of a pie plate that sting people in shallow water in California and Mexico. These suckers were huge, easily the size of a card table, weighing over one hundred pounds with a six-or seven-foot tail armed with a six-inch-long barb.

The first one I saw was in 1956 when my father speared one. He had seen them several years earlier and made a special spear for going after them. It was about nine feet long, with a single point and large barbs that came out after the spear entered the fish. He swam out and speared the smallest one in the school. The next thing he knew, he was being towed through the water. Then a guard boat came out to get him, and it was towed through the water with him and the two guards in it. Finally, the ray got tired enough so they could row to the beach. Just as they hit the shorebreak, they flipped. Somehow, my father managed to hold onto the rope attached to the spear without getting stung.

The next thing we saw was him dragging this huge stingray up the beach with its tail flying all over the place looking for something or someone to sink its barb into. Of course the tourists had to come running up to get a close look at the show. With a lot of yelling, my father managed to keep the tourists back and get the ray to a large post where he was able to haul it up. Later he took it to a nearby market, and it weighed in at eighty-five pounds. And he said it was the smallest one in the school.

Scariest Moment

RAY B. ('55-'60) - I remember it real clear. Bobby Mrozek was with me and, I think, Ed Verna. It was before the season. We were cleaning the beach on Brown Avenue. We were raking up beach debris. There was a bunch of kids from a grammar school. They had brought them down for a day trip to their summer home. Like typical kids, they ran down the beach, dropping their towels as they ran. They went in, right into a nice calm *run*. They hit that thing and *bam*! Off they go! There was a kid, about sixteen years old, he was like their chaperone. He went in after them and got two of them out, then he went in for two more. Consequently, we were there. We went out, but there was more than one kid per person. We didn't feel the cold water because the adrenalin was pumping, but we weren't in shape like we were in August. After all, we had been drinking beer in college. We ended up breaking all the lifesaving rules—like don't let them grab you around the neck—but what are you going to do with two kids? Dick K. (a municipal utilities man) was on the beach. We sent him down to get some apparatus. He went down there to get it and then started to look around. Damn if that nitwit forgot what he was there for. He wasn't illiterate because nobody hadn't tried to teach him—he couldn't learn. He needed help to play a jukebox. Meanwhile, we're moving out and just trying to stay afloat. We stayed calm and then made it in by hitting another sandbar. The kids had no adults present.

People come down and go right to the dangerous spots. "Oh, that place looks nice. There's no waves there, let's go there."

Rescuing A Mummy

MIKE H. - I was guarding in Ortley sometime in the 1950s when a guy and his kid walked into the water. The guy was wrapped from head to toe in bandages, kind of like a mummy. He had some type of skin problem and his doctor told him that it would be good for him to soak in saltwater. Unfortunately, he was a weak swimmer, and he and his son got caught in a little rip. Nothing serious, so I went out with a torpedo to bring them in. By the time I got out to him, his bandages had unraveled and become soaked with water. They got wrapped around me, him, and his kid. What started out as a simple little pull became a major effort. The bandages got in my face, around my head, neck, and arms while the guy and his kid were panicking. It took a lot of effort to just breathe and get them into the beach with all the soaked bandages weighing me down.

Big Hair Rescue

MIKE H. - I went out to get a guy and a girl caught in a rip one day in the 1950s. It was a pretty good-sized day, and they were out a ways. He was doing okay, but she was pretty panicked. She had a bathing cap on, which was not that unusual in those days. I started bringing them in when her bathing cap popped off as we got hit by some waves. It turned out that inside that cap she had hair that was so long it almost reached her ankles. The hair got wrapped around my head, and I almost drowned before I could get my face free. Once again, what seemed like a simple routine rescue turned into a major struggle.

Power Rowing

RAY B. - The Whale was a beach cop first, then became a guard.

Bob Mrozek and I worked at adjacent beaches. The Whale would take the stern, Bob would take the bow, and I would take the middle. People said a cop shouldn't go out in the boat, so we convinced The Whale he should be a guard.

He was magnificently strong. He was so powerful, that when the boat was dead in the water and he needed to get it going, he'd snap the oars—he'd have two stumps in his hands. He had to deliberately try not to break the oars. Usually you got three or four years out of a set of oars, but they broke in less than two years with him.

Captain Mystery

RAY B. - Jackie Homer, the captain of the guards, was a big influence on all of us. Jackie had a skin diving business and would go off on a diving job. You never knew where he was going to turn up. He'd come out of the water in his scuba gear, he'd fly by in a plane, and he'd come by water skiing behind a speedboat. He was wonderful. This dispatcher would get the calls for Jack, and then he ended up looking around for him. He was captain for three to four years.

Crank Calls

RAY B. - Back in the '50s, we had Army phones. A crank turned a magneto that rang the bell, which required a fair amount of voltage, which was why this thing was manual. It had four C dry cell batteries. They were in series. All the bells on all the phones rang at one time, and everyone could listen at the same time. We used to have sing-a-longs.

The phones had brass wires to connect with the lugs. If you were connecting or disconnecting the contacts when it got rung, you got a nick—a shock. I worked with Ritchie Wenzel most of the years. He had a good pair of expensive binoculars, and every night we would watch when guys called in to shut down at the end of the day. Bob Mrozek was at the next beach, or Eddie Verna with Dick Hoffman. We'd sit there every night, one of us with binoculars, the other at the crank, and say, "Get ready...get ready..." And when the one with the binoculars saw them start to loosen the lugs, he'd say "Now!" And we'd get 'em. We did this night after night. "We got'em again!"

When disconnecting the wires, nobody would think of using something like a handkerchief or some kind of light insulation—we were too dumb for that.

One time there were these three pesky kids that were hanging around the stand. So one of the guards asked us to ring the line as he held it against one of the kids. Nothing happened. He tried it again. Nothing. Finally the guard touched the wires—and we cranked the phone. Zap! *He* got it!

Beach Ponds

MIKE H. - Sometimes when there was a high berm in the front of the beach, and a large swell and a high tide, the water would rush over the berm and create a pool in the middle of the beach. This did not happen very often, but when it did, it was a real treat for the kids. The pools were never more than eighteen inches deep, but would sometimes be over two hundred feet long.

Eventually, enough water would build up and begin to drain at one end of the pool. The ensuing erosion would often create a small set of rapids across the berm, back into the ocean. You had to watch out for little kids playing near that end of the pool because they could easily get sucked into the rapids and washed into the ocean. If the kids did get washed out of the pool, they could be facing some nasty shorebreaks. On top of that, rips often formed where these pools drained and that could make it even more serious when a kid got caught.

Before The Jetties

ARCHIE M. ('58-'64) - Back then, we had the ropes and the poles. People had a knack for getting caught up in them, particularly when the current was really running. Before the jetties were put in, the currents were really strong—like a river.

An Air-Borne Victim

ARCHIE M. - I remember we were all out on a pull—about fourteen guards. It was a terrible day: the waves must have been ten-feet high. Eddie Verna and someone else went out in the lifeguard boat. It was almost comical, but it wasn't. They pulled this victim into the lifeguard boat. Coming in, I don't know what happened, whether he took a wave in or what, but he buried the nose coming down the wave, and of course, the boat flipped. It catapulted this kid out of the boat; you could see the kid in the air. Then it took a whole new crew to go out there and bring them in again. And Eddie—Eddie broke his nose and everybody was bleeding. There must have been at least fourteen guards in the water with ropes and everything. Probably pulled in two or three people.

There were times when we would pull out thirty people in the course of a day.

Dunes at Island Beach State Park. This photo, taken in 2004, evokes the early landscape of the Jersey Shore. A short distance from Lavallette, the park's ten and a half mile length is almost in the same pristine condition as when Henry Hudson sailed the region. It is one of the few remaining undeveloped barrier beaches on the North Atlantic.

Fiberglass surfboats began to replace the more expensive wooden boats in the '60s and '70s. This one, most likely a Van Dyne, is equipped for competition with seat braces and high oarlocks. While more buoyant in the water, fiberglass boats are harder to control in rough surf.

June
Expectations

The salty breeze off the frigid ocean carries a brighter bouquet and an electric charge in June. It stirs a sense of freedom and possibilities that seem to permeate the last throes of spring. High school students prepare for graduation, a summer of fun, and anticipation of college. College students have nearly the entire month to party, make arrangements for living at the beach, and enjoy the reprieve from term papers.

It is also when lifeguard tests are administered to confirm the fitness—or lack thereof—of the candidates who would take their place on the white benches that would dot the beaches.

The would-be lifeguards may have any combination of a handful of motives for seeking the work: prestige, tradition, love of the ocean, exhibitionism, parties, pursuit of the opposite sex, a break from the mental rigors of college, or simply, an easy paycheck and a good tan.

Those that pass the test are not always selected. Small communities tend to give preferential treatment to their favorite sons and daughters and discourage those they do not know well or those with a perceived blot on their reputation. This is where the captain of guards and his lieutenants can begin to shape the character of their beach patrol squad. Troublemakers, defined in a variety of ways, are culled out. Those with whom they share values are drawn in.

Once the selection is made, the pairing of partners and beach assignments is decided. Usually, the most seasoned guards are paired with the greenest of rookies. Sometimes bench partners are paired for the entire summer; other times it lasts only for a week. Captains strive for balance on each beach, mating the more experienced or more diligent with the eager but untested rookies.

The beaches in Lavallette are numbered, beginning with Beach #1 at the north end of town. For much of its history, Lavallette has had six ocean beaches and two bay beaches. In the 1960s, other unguarded beach areas were set aside for surfing.

Each beach has distinct traits. The people, the society, the currents, and the sandbars all can vary throughout the season. All summer long, one beach may have no rescues while another has them weekly, even daily.

The bathing areas have been marked off by several methods over the years. Thick, trimmed cedar poles, fifteen feet high, used to be jetted into the sandbars and on the beach. Then one-inch thick hemp line was tied from the pole in the water to the one on the beach. Children and elderly people would often hold onto these ropes for support as they entered the water. Later, lines were attached by anchors and the poles on the beach were replaced with stakes. Most recently, only white flags on the beach mark the north and south borders of the bathing areas.

Assignments for guarding partners are usually rotated every week or two. It cuts down on complaints from people who feel that they have been stuck with lousy guards, provides guarding equity, and helps to insure that equipment is checked regularly and maintained.

The gear varies from one beach patrol to another, but the "tools of the trade" are basically the same: a tall bench, a first aid kit, torpedo buoys, rescue line, a large rescueboard, and a surfboat. Recently, rescue kayaks and backboards have become commonplace.

The seven-foot high bench gives the guards a commanding view of the water and beach and provides a place to stow first aid kits, jackets, towels, lost-and-found items, sun protection, and radios. It also provides a place to hang torpedo buoys and wet clothing. Blackboards on the back of the stands usually post the beach number, guards names, water temperature, tide times, and occasionally, bathing guidelines.

The first aid kits usually include sun shield, gauze, band-aids, hydrogen peroxide, first aid cream, tweezers, and scissors. In recent years, latex gloves have been added to the supplies. Splinters, mostly from the boardwalks, are the most common injuries. Many youngsters are convinced that a Band-Aid from a lifeguard will have magical properties and make even the smallest cut better.

The torpedo buoys—sometimes called cans or torps—may be made of metal, foam rubber, or high-impact plastic. They are delivered to distressed people to keep them afloat and tow them ashore. Torpedo buoys can keep several people up in an emergency. The cans have clips to accept rescue line, if necessary, and are often connected by a trailing line to the heavy brass ring on the leather and canvas belts worn by some guards. The rescue line is rarely used except when the current is extremely strong—usually after a storm at sea.

The rescue boards—basically a tandem surfboard with rope handles—are used mostly for patrolling beach areas, but they can be very effective when a rescue involves numerous victims. Under the right circumstances, they enable a guard to reach victims extremely quickly.

The surfboats may be made of wood or fiberglass. The wood boats cut through rough surf without getting tossed about as much as the lighter but faster fiberglass boats. Wood boats are dwindling in numbers now; the craft of making them is dying out as the craftsmen age and retire—in some cases leaving no heir to preserve the lore and wis-

dom of their craft.

The surfboats are designed for two rowers, although one experienced rower can get through mild surf without much trouble. Two rowers must work as a team or the boat may become a deadly weapon, mowing down bathers and guards alike. It is not uncommon to hear profanity issuing from one of these boats as it bursts through waves or rides the surf.

Once they get to their assigned beach, the rookies begin to learn that the Red Cross Senior Lifesaving certification is just the beginning of becoming a lifeguard.

▲ ▲ ▲

Reason For Life Guarding

RUSSELL F. ('50-'51) - You could sit on the stand, and the girls looked up to you. That is the number one, prime reason for lifeguarding.

Physical Description Of Lavallette Beach

From the Lavallette Beach Patrol Lifeguard Manual, n.d.:

The Lavallette Bathing Beach is a 1.5-mile stretch of Atlantic coastline located in the northern portion of Ocean County between Ocean Beach I and Ortley Beach. The northerly boundary is the wood snow fence placed across the beach, and the southern boundary is 50 yards south of the rock jetty at Dover Avenue indicated by snow fence. The westerly boundary of the beach is defined by a wooden boardwalk. Entrance to the beach is gained via stairs and ramps. Nine bathing areas are operated within the natural beach divisions created by the rock groins. White beach flags placed at the high water mark define actual bathing areas.

The normal beach width varies from 50 to 75 yards depending upon tides, wind conditions, storms, etc. Bathing area bottoms are normally stable, dropping away gradually to a water depth of 20' to 200' from the waters edge at high tide [sic].

There are consistent sandbars, and rip conditions may occur.

Two bathing areas are located on the Barnegat Bay at Reese and Washington Avenues. Actual bathing areas are defined by buoy supported ropes extending outward, approximately 75 yards in width. Bathing area bottom conditions are stable, sloping gradually to a water depth of six feet.

Growing Up In Lavallette

GORDON H. ('65-'73, '75) - Lavallette is part of a barrier island—originally just a sandbar that developed a system of dunes. It is flanked on the east by the Atlantic, and on the west by the mile-wide Barnegat Bay. In most places, the distance between the ocean and the bay is less than half a mile. During major storms and hurricanes, the ocean waves wash over the dunes and bulkheads facing the beach and drain into the bay. Often homes in their way are destroyed.

When I was a child, there were large dunes at the end of my street. They got trampled and cut down when the boardwalk was extended in the late 1950s. We lived only several hundred feet from the ocean. At night, from my bed, the hushed crash of the waves played a mantra prelude to wonderful dreams.

In the winter, Lavallette was a ghost resort town with a population of five hundred. The kindergarten through eighth grade grammar school had so few students that one teacher taught two or three grade levels at a time. I think at one point, the entire grammar school had four teachers. As a child, I longed for the companionship that summer would bring. During the summer, little Lavallette, not even an entire square mile in size, contained a population in the tens of thousands.

The beaches along this portion of the Jersey Shore (I am told by people who have traveled the world and swam in its oceans) are among the finest on the planet. The waters are usually very safe and the currents gentle; beneath the water, the sandy bottom rarely has harmful elements. The white beach sand is composed of large grains that hold their shape well for sand castles and body chairs. To my sensibilities, the sand is "soft." Some have even called it "fluffy."

The bayberry bushes that grew almost everywhere when I was a child gave off a mild, sweet aroma in the late summer. Back then, most of the homes were small cottages built during post-World War II prosperity. Few were more than unfinished stud walls with screened in porches to hold the marsh mosquitoes at bay. If the homes had any heat at all, it was often kerosene or a fireplace that burned driftwood.

The death knell of summer always came on Labor Day. That Monday was a time of sharp transition and melancholy. On Labor Day morning, the streets were filled with the cars of friends and their families. By bittersweet evening, the streets were barren, with only a few cars. It seemed that the whole world had abandoned me and returned to the bustle of New York and northern New Jersey. Many friends I would not see for nine months, if ever again.

A Child Of The Dunes

ANDY B. ('65-'70) - Growing up in Lavallette in the '50s was an idyllic, if somewhat sheltered, experience. One woke up and fell asleep to the sound of the surf. The tiny peninsula in those days was not covered with concrete and asphalt, condo complexes, and three-story homes built within three feet of the property lines.

The locals typically lived in small, converted bungalows tucked into lots that were covered with bayberry, beach plum, small pines, and cherry trees. Children grew up in close contact with the natural habitat and followed the flow of the seasons: fishing, hunting and trapping small game in the fall and winter, and spending endless hours honing their body surfing and swimming skills during the summer. When the surf was up, entire days would be spent treading water outside the breakers, waiting for the Big One to build up outside.

The lifeguards seemed more benevolent and were acquainted with the locals and usually left us alone, sometimes even joining us. The big thrill was, of course, the September surf with its huge, beautifully shaped waves emanating long distances to the Jersey Shore from the hurricane waters of the South Atlantic. To hang onto a really big wave without becoming buried in foam and tossed to the bottom was a major achievement. It was said that if one looked up while on the crest of a really big wave, one could look across the half-mile wide peninsula and see Barnegat Bay, clearly visible over the rooftops.

On The Beach

GORDON H. - I had practically grown up on the ocean beaches of Lavallette. When I was old enough to be trusted to walk on the beach alone—probably when I was about nine, I used to beachcomb for hours after school when the weather was good. After storms, I would search for the treasures of bottles from the shipping lanes and other flotsam. I discovered how different tides would bring in whole varieties of aquatic life—calico crabs, sea robins, starfish, and a myriad of different jellyfish.

In the summer, I would spend every hour possible in the water— swimming, diving, snorkeling, rafting, and body surfing. I loved the action of the waves, the sensual wash of bubbles, and the prospect of shell treasures waiting to be discovered under the surface. In the evening, I would join beach buddies on the cool sand for football and baseball games, usually coming home in the darkness with sand coating my hair and in my ears and underwear.

Over the years, I began to take more notice of the guards and to learn the names of those that returned year after year. They became the embodiment of the best that I thought a young adult could be. They were great athletic swimmers, got to take out the surfboat, and got a lot of attention from women. A few were even friendly to me and made me feel important. They seemed like minor gods.

When I reached my teens, I felt that I would not be complete if I did not lifeguard at some point in my life. I would eventually guard for nine years on three New Jersey beaches and one year in Florida.

Andy and I

GORDON H. - We seemed fated to become friends. We were born on the same day, with Andy arriving just a few hours ahead of me. We met in the second grade. Around fourth grade, we discovered we shared the same birthday and that seemed to make us even better friends—we were sort of like twins, even though we did not look a bit alike.

As the years went by, we shared such experiences as the same teachers in high school, going out for the baseball and football teams together, and registering for the draft. Other parallels would arise as we continued through life. We spent so much time together and shared so many of the same sensibilities that we developed a verbal shorthand. We could have conversations where outsiders could understand only a portion of our elliptical verbal riffs and coded shorthand expressions. This speech jazz had the buzz of camaraderie.

Andy's father and uncle had both been lifeguards on the beach in our town. His father was a decorated Marine pilot in World War II—a bona fide hero who had fought at Midway. I always thought Andy hoped to earn some respect from his father by being a lifeguard.

Apprenticing In The Surfboat

GORDON H. - Andy's father bought two beat-up surfboats that the borough did not want to repair. The wood was dried out, and the seams were cracking. Andy fixed up the better of the two, and in the spring, before the lifeguard tryouts, Andy and I would go out in the surf and row the length of town and back, stopping along the way to bail the water that had trickled in. We were only seventeen, but full of hope to get our spindlely, one hundred sixty pound frames in shape, be competent in the lifeboats, and pass the lifeguard tryouts.

Because we were inexperienced, in the beginning we clashed every time we went out in the boat. Usually we had trouble matching the tempo of strokes, and the man in the stern seat would get the handle ends of the oars in his back. When one rower fell out of sync with the other, the oars would hit each other and usually bounce out of the oar-locks. This crippled the boat, and it usually happened at the worst times—like when a wave was bearing down on us.

To effectively go through breaking waves requires that the oars be in the water pulling toward the onrushing hill of water. If the oars were not stabilizing the boat when the wave hit, or the boat did not have enough momentum, it could quickly be turned by the wave, making it vulnerable to successive waves in the set.

Cursing, accusations, and panicked yells issued from the boat. The subject of body eliminations was mentioned and symbolically acted upon in one-word oratories.

We worked hard at developing a smooth, powerful rhythm with the oars. After coaching from Andy's father and uncle, we began to get the knack for feathering the oars—rolling the blades to the horizontal position in the air, twisting them for a good "bite" on the water, and snapping an extra kick at the very end of the stroke. When we got good at following the same rhythm, we began to pick up the pace. To feel the boat surge forward with the combined power and confidence we began to develop was invigorating. We were in the process of physically becoming men. As our calluses grew and we improved, often we would get intoxicated with the giddy thrill of the boat slicing through the brisk water in harmony with our backs, legs, arms, and hands.

Boat Surfing

GORDON H. - Gaining the skill to ride waves to shore in the boat was much harder than rowing out through breaking surf. Along with coordinated rowing, it requires a series of discrete and accelerating actions, agility, and precise timing. First, the boat has to be in the right location and direction relative to the wave. The goal is to be at the right spot in the wave's development and moving fast enough when the wave reaches you that you begin to coast with it. Then the stern rower has to ship his oars and nimbly leap to the very stern of the boat with an oar and use it as a tiller. In the meantime, the bow rower has to row furiously to keep the boat "in" the wave.

If the stern rower did not move toward the stern directly over the center of the keel, the boat easily began to veer to one side and risk broaching (rolling over). If you were not going parallel to the wave's path, or aimed in the same direction as its shoulder, there were several ways to "bail out" of the wave. You could back oar, have both rowers go to the stern to make the boat plane inefficiently, have the stern rower hang off the stern and drag his body like a "sea anchor," or both rowers could lean into the gunnel on the wave side of the boat.

Andy and I spent as much time as we could during the spring of our senior year in high school in the surfboat, usually going out after school or on the weekends. Our confidence grew each time we went out, but we still had trouble mastering wave riding in the boat.

Early on one gorgeous June afternoon, just one or two days before our high school graduation, we took the boat out, rowed about a mile, and began to ride waves. The water was pristine and in the sixties. As the tide began to come in, the waves began to carry more volume and take nice shape—the largest were about three feet. Had we been more experienced, we might have noticed that the sandbar came up fast and was very high. This made the waves build very fast and crash hard.

We took off on one of the biggest waves of the day—a four-footer—and we were aimed right along its shoulder. Then things went wrong. In an instant, we dropped down into the breaking part of the wave, and it folded on the boat, rolling it over. As it struck the high sandbar, the gunnel cracked out of the aged hull. Both Andy and I were under the boat when it split up. We now were under a two hundred pound piece of wreckage, with its twelve inch, dagger-sharp rib fingers floating above us as another wave washed over. I cleared the wreckage and looked for Andy. He lay face down in the wash, and bloody welts scored his back where the surfboat's jagged ribs had scraped and clawed over him. I feared the worst as I splashed toward him and grabbed his arm. He snapped to his feet.

"I was waiting for it to wash over me," he said slightly dazed.

"We're lucky to be alive," I said.

We both felt a few moments of exhilaration from the camaraderie of a close call. Then we gathered the pieces of the hull and pulled them ashore. As we did, we began to fill with doubt that we had done something wrong to wreck the boat. And we wondered if word of the wreck might jeopardize our chances at the lifeguard tryouts in just a few days.

Bad Boat On The Sandbar

ANDY B. - When I was seventeen, Dad and I purchased an old Hankins boat, and I spent the winter in our garage refurbishing it. I wanted to have it ready by early spring so I could sharpen my skills in preparation for the June lifeguard tryouts. By April, I had the relic in reasonably good shape and ready for launching. Every day after school, one of my friends and I (usually fellow guard-candidate Gordon Hesse) would row the boat out through the surf and spend an hour or more building our skill and endurance pulling on a pair of cumbersome, nine-foot oars. Although we became proficient at rowing, our wave riding skills left much to be desired. Several days before the test, we were making some fledgling attempts at surfboating with Gordon in the rear and me in the bow. We were doing it all wrong. I was jumping to the bow after shipping oars, and Gordon would sit on the transom without the tiller oar trying to influence the direction of the boat by shifting his weight. This was fine on the small, shapeless waves, but this time, when we caught a five-footer with a crest and well-defined belly, the bow of the boat immediately went down and to the left, the boat going sideways and then capsizing. The compression of the wave snapped the boat neatly in two, with the jagged edges of the broken ribs raking my back as I lay on the bottom.

Two days later, in great embarrassment and to the great amusement of all the veterans, I went to my first tryout with those red stripes clearly visible across my back. I remember Captain Dick Ginglen coming up to me as I prepared to launch the town's boat for the rowing portion of the test and begging me to be careful because the town could not afford to lose a $900.00 boat every time I took one out. I smiled sheepishly while the old boys roared in approval. It was some consolation that I held my own in the boat portion of the tryouts and did well enough in the swim events to gain a spot on the roster for the 1965 season.

Early Lifeguard Auditions

RUSSELL F. - I was sixteen when I started guarding. They needed guards, and I was a tall kid. Old man Goddard hired me—he was the captain of the guards back then. He said, "Can you swim?" I said "yeah" and got the job.

My first bench partner was Frank Perkins. He was a short guy. He always walked on his toes so he'd look taller. I was down at the bay most of the time—it was tough to kill the boredom. I just watched the mothers. There wasn't much hazing unless you screwed up.

Trial By Ice

TOM A. ('63-'70) - Actually, the first test we took to guard in Bay Head was given by Harry Niehms in Lavallette. The year before, all the Bay Head lifeguards had gone on strike, so they fired them: it was a case of which came first, the chicken or the egg. So we got up for the tryouts. It's May or early June, the ocean is about fifty-four degrees, maybe. One of us has to swim out and be the victim, then the other swims out and has to rescue him. Then they switched and the other one had to swim out and be the victim. So you had to go in twice. I was never so cold in my life. Jumped in the water and my brother Jimmy looked like he was swimming backwards. Every muscle in my body started to tighten up. We got back to the beach, and Jimmy immediately went to the back of the beach and threw up. I was always proud of the fact that I didn't throw up. I thought I was going to die, but I didn't throw up.

When I had to take the test for Lavallette, Jimmy said, "I'm never going to take the test again." He couldn't take the cold water anymore. For him, seventy degrees isn't warm enough. Now they take the test in a pool? Bunch of wussies!

Lifeguard Tryouts

GORDON H. - My first lifeguard tryout involved competing with about forty young men for about twenty-six positions. Probably slightly more than half the people trying out had already guarded, so it was assumed they had to screw up not to get a position. The test consisted of a timed swim, a short dash on the beach followed by running into the water and rescuing a "victim" about one hundred fifty feet offshore, and rowing the surfboat out to a buoy and back. We probably had to do a surfboard rescue as well.

I don't recall the tryout as being extremely physically challenging other than the water temperature was fifty-six degrees Fahrenheit. The cold water only made me want to swim faster so I could get out of it. One team flipped the surfboat over as they brought it into the shore-break on the beach, narrowly missing serious injury.

After tabulating the scores, the names of those selected were called out, and we were issued two bright red guard swim trunks, strap tee shirts, an Acme Thunderer whistle, and a leather and canvas belt with a large brass clip ring. Later we were assigned our bench partner and beach assignments.

As rookies, Andy got assigned to Roger, and I worked on an adjacent beach with Sam. We were assigned to veteran guards who were good friends. By our second and third years, there was enough experience on the beaches that we were made bench partners for most of the season.

Spring Thaw

JIMMY A. ('66-'67) - In '66, the water for the lifeguard test was incredibly cold. You literally dreaded going in the water. I spent an hour in a hot tub afterward trying to get my body warm. It was unbelievably cold.

Primary Colors

TOM A. - First day in Bay Head—I was proud as a peacock. It was a nice day, and it was early in the season. I'm sitting there all day. I had no idea how burned I was going to get. The next day, I could hardly get out of bed. I was sitting with a blanket all over me with a big hat. I don't think I got any sun for the rest of the summer. Being up high on the stand, you're cooler—there's always a breeze. I had never bothered to put a shirt on or cover myself. It's amazing to me that every one of us doesn't have skin cancer. We had that zinc oxide that made us all look like clowns. It was bad enough when you had it on your nose, but when you put it on your lips, you really looked bad.

Years later, after I was married, I would come home and be really tired. And my wife would say, "What are you tired for? All you did was sit in the sun all day." Now she sits on the beach all day and says she's tired. Oh, *really?!*

Going Through The Motions

GORDON H. - The second year I guarded, Sam gave me a lecture at a party a couple of nights before the lifeguard test. He said something like, "Now we pretty much have our jobs sewn up, so we don't have to knock ourselves out on the lifeguard test. Let's just stay together so nobody looks bad." The next day we had a run-swim event. And they matched me up with Sam. I just couldn't hold back and built a good lead on him before entering the water. He probably never forgave me.

Fog Honeys

MICKEY H. ('67-'76) - Guarding in June could often be cold and lonely. Some days we would sit there when the air and water would be cold and there would be a thick fog. You could not see more than two hundred feet, and it was damp. No one would be in the water, and there would be almost no girls to check out. Every now and then some would go walking by in sweatsuits. Tommy M. used to refer to them as fog honeys. They could really help to keep you going on a slow, uncomfortable day.

Side Money

JIM C. ('67-present; Captain '81-present) - In the late '70s, a lot of times it was like we were hiring guards because they were good softball players. There was a time when softball was a big thing. There were leagues; we had championships. We'd even make more money— or as much money—playing a game of softball. You know, playing $2.00 or $3.00 a man, sometimes even $5.00 a man—it got pretty competitive. So you're making $1.10 or $1.25 to $1.50 an hour as a lifeguard, and you could go down there and play a game of softball for a couple of bucks. It got to be you'd bet against the opposing guy—I play left field, you play left field. All right, whoever wins, 'You pay me.'

Then it got to be where there was a league and standings. We had big crowds down there at nighttime watching the softball games. It got to be a pretty competitive thing.

Years before, in fact, we used to have a keg right there on the sidelines. It used to be you played for a keg of beer.

Gearing Up

ANDY B. - "Andy, Dick Ginglen just came by on his bike. One of the guards has been injured, and they need you to start right away." It was my mother. She had crossed the street to the laundry where I had languished and sweated away the summers of my youth, marking time until starting my new lifeguard job at the official opening of the season on June 26, 1965.

So my change in careers came abruptly as I jogged the seven blocks to the lifeguard headquarter's trailer.

I was quickly issued the standard equipment: two size thirty-six red cotton bathing suits—the only available size (which looked vaguely like a ballerina skirt on my 6'2", 153 pound frame), two white muscle-tee shirts, an Acme Thunderer whistle, a canvas and leather life-saving belt with a brass ring, and a heavy blue wool overcoat.

After a quick change in the bathroom, and taking note of the fact that my skinny white body did not in the least resemble a lifeguard's, uniform or not, I continued jogging to my assigned post at Beach #4 on New Brunswick Avenue. Lugging my coat, extra uniform, and my street clothes, I must have looked as ridiculous as I was frightened.

First Bench Partner

ANDY B. - I arrived at the Beach #4 stand huffing and puffing and frazzled when I was greeted by a muscular and imposing figure, meso-morphic in stature, with a face that was naturally comical: a big, broad nose with close-set, heavy-lidded eyes, and brown hair, close-cropped in the style of the day. His voice was a thick, almost syrupy, southern drawl. The picture of virile manhood was shattered by the fact that he was wearing a heavy, white wool sock over a bandaged foot.

"Way'll, you must be Andy, my name's Frank D," he said. "Don be sha, c'mon climb aboard." A hand with an iron grip reached out and pulled me up on the high chair. "Ahm hangin' around 'til Rogie gets back from lunch. You can see my foot's a little messed up, and you'll be takin' mah place. Ya never done this b'fore? Get up and ah'll fill ya in on the basics."

For the next half hour, I listened intently as Frank D., a.k.a. "Duke," imparted lifeguard wisdom of the ages.

"The trick, Andy, is to keep the folks within the ropes, crowded together," he patiently explained. "Sounds awful, but it makes life real easy. That way, you just have to watch the bathers on the outside. If anybody in close here gets in trouble, one of the other swimmers will help'm. It's when an outside swimmer gets in trouble or drifts off in a run that you got a problem. All the bathers should be kept within one hundred yards or so of the stand. If they're too far away, you'll never reach them before they go under."

"Watch their faces. Anybody in trouble will always be looking at the beach for help. Y'all never see'em looking away. Look for that scared look on their face, and see if they're strugglin' or tired. Most people are too proud to wave fer help. Ya have ta look fer the little signs."

And on and on, a wealth of basic common sense knowledge was quickly imparted. The initiation had begun.

The Penalty Box

BOB G. ('63-'67, '69) - The bay beach was considered the "penalty box."

Low Man On The Totem Pole

SAM H. ('62-'68) - I started on the bay and stayed there the whole summer. There were only three new guards that year so they put two of the rookies, Dick A. and myself, on the bay. They knew Wayne B., so he got to the ocean beach. They weren't worried about putting inexperienced people on the bay because we could always wade.

All I remember about working on the bay was they were dredging. I'd row my little rowboat around. The boat had about two planks. The only time I got to the ocean was when somebody got punished.

The first time I was ever on the ocean—somebody got punished—they stuck me with Eddie Verna and Ralph Krone. That was a great experience. Ralph went for lunch at about 10:30 and came back a couple hours later; Eddie V. went for lunch for a couple of hours, and I went out for a couple of hours. When I got back they said, "Gosh, we forgot to call you out, you can go back out."

The following year, I got on the beach full time. Arnie K. was captain at the time. My first year on the ocean beach, I worked with Wayne B. He was the one who really broke me in. He was a great partner. He could really swim. But don't tell him I said that.

Tight Ships

JIMMY A. - I was broke in by Joe M. Joe literally hated rafts. It was just something else to watch. A lot of parents would buy rafts for their kids, and they couldn't swim. No matter how calm the water, he wanted no rafts.

Master Of His Domain

ARCHIE M. ('58-'64) - George K., he played for the Vikings for a while. Long hair was coming in. George was Mr. Clean—shaved head and the whole bit. He used to terrorize these kids. He used to call these kids up to the stand and chase them off his beach until they got haircuts.

The First Woman Guard

BOB G. - The first woman guard in Lavallette was Janey Ford—I think it was probably around '62 or '63.

The Perfect Job

PATRICIA D. ('67-'69) - When I started I thought, 'This is a great summer job. This is what I want to do for the summer. I've still got nights off, I still get a day off, and I get to spend the day at the beach.'

At the bay, in some senses, I was a glorified babysitter. I really didn't get to read much because the parents would drop off kids. I don't think I could have done the ocean part.

Starting The Day On The Beach

DICK H. ('50-2000; Captain '66-'80) - The main thing in the morning is to eye the water before you get on the stand to figure out what you were going to do and where you were going to let them go.

First Year Hazing

ANDY B. - That first year, 1965, (and despite the fact that I spent a good deal of time under the tutelage of Duke), Roger K. was my assigned bench partner. Although he had only one season under his belt and was only a year my senior, to my adolescent perception he may as well have been thirty. To me, he was all things that I lacked: worldly, witty, confident, and good looking. Although the mists of passing time have dimmed many memories and obliterated others, Roger stands out in my memory with the clarity of a polished diamond. In my limited understanding of charisma, all I could comprehend about Roger was that he was fun to be around and dominated situations, not the other way around. He and Duke took me under their wings, and as I came to understand, the fact that they treated me as a fraternity pledge and busted my balls unmercifully was their way of displaying acceptance and even a sort of friendship. I learned if the older guys didn't like you, you were simply ignored. Duke and Roger soon evolved an entire comedy sketch based on their contention that I was a closet homosexual. Roger's nickname for me was "Fop." Eventually, it was refined into "Fopster," in lieu of a Viking name such as Lobster.

Roger and Duke decided to embark on a mission to make a man out of me and get me involved with women. I recall one day when I remained dateless for one of the rare and infamous island party rituals.

The party was that night. Duke was intent on getting me a date. He scanned the beach all day and finally spotted a seventeen-year old blonde. He summoned her to the stand and introduced himself—and then me—as a respectable young man who, through some incredible misfortune, was dateless for a very important lifeguard party. To my joy and disbelief, she bought Duke's line and agreed to accompany me. Duke then gave me a set of detailed instructions on how I should conduct myself in order to come off as smooth and sophisticated, concluding his remarks with the stern admonition: "Andee, you don't have a hair on yer ass if you don't strap that little girl down."

Needless to say, I didn't get to first base that night, and it was with great trepidation that I showed my face at work the next day to face my mentor. Duke waited until we were all set up and sitting on the bench before starting his inquisition.

With feigned disinterest, scratching his chin and looking at the sky, he casually asked, "Sooo, Andee, hoow did ya make out on yer big date last naight?"

"Oh, I had an okay time, Duke."

Duke suddenly became intense: "Did ya get any..." he dropped one eyebrow and his eyes darted left and right as if to make sure there were no ease droppers, "...pussy?!"

Me, after a pregnant pause: "Yea, actually I did."

"Ya did?!" His excitement was palpable.

"Well, yea, after I got home I got so frustrated 'cause the bitch wouldn't kiss me that I snuck out and raped the neighbor's cat."

Duke exploded: "Oh, Jesus, oh, Christ, that's good. *Ha, ha, ha*, wait 'til I tell Dick..." Quickly he got on the phone to the lieutenant. "Hey Dick, guess what Andee jus tol me?!"

First Rescue

ARCHIE M. - I remember my first pull. I was up on the stand—Mr. Macho—I had my hat on and the stuff underneath my eyes. The time came to go rescue a victim, and I ran like hell down the beach. It was low tide—and I almost hit the water—then I remembered I had my hat on. Rather than throwing it off, I turned around and ran all the way back to the stand. I put my hat on the stand before heading back to the water because I was a nervous wreck.

Fish Names

GORDON H. - Veteran lifeguards would often give themselves romantic nautical names—like "The Whale" or "Cuda"—that evoked their behavior, style, or weight class—either of Viking or aquatic origin. Sam used "Leif," his buddy was "Erik," and John T. was "Thor." "Shark" and "Dolphin" were but a few others. Part of the annual hazing ritual one year was to give derogatory names to the rookies— particularly those that were considered marginally good guards. One fellow by the name of Snider (who had wasted no time in establishing himself as an undesirable bench partner) was hissingly referred to as "Jewfish." Andy was threatened to become "Blowfish" if he did not follow the hazing whims of his senior partner. Of course, this naming was taken up by the less clever sophomore lifeguards and degenerated to names like "Jellyfish" and "Turdfish."

Issued Equipment

SAM H. - One year they told us we could buy whatever kind of hat we wanted. So they did that only for one year because we all came back with all these dopey hats. Fricchone came back with one of those Mexican hats they use for a hat dance—all it lacked was those little fuzzy balls hanging all around it.

My First Partner

GORDON H. - I was lucky. I drew Sam, a great partner to "break" me in. He had more experience on the squad than anyone other than the captain and one other guard. He had a round face, long legs on a high-waisted frame, and longish blond hair that made me think of a haystack. I think he was twenty-three and had guarded for five years. He was a seasoned pro. The son of a physician, he was personable and played down his intelligence. He was also mischievous—what some people would call a "smart ass." He was an English major at West Virginia University.

Although I was green and had only just turned eighteen, I knew enough to know that I did not know very much. I tried to keep my mouth shut except to ask questions, and I tried to make them sensible enough to warrant a response. Sam did not seem to mind the endless stream of questions I put to him about lifeguarding and life in general.

On my first day on the beach with Sam, the importance of the job hit me. Along with him, I was responsible for everyone on the beach. The idea that someone could die due to my negligence or inexperience dawned on me, and I vowed that I would not be the first guard in Lavallette's history to let someone drown while I was on duty.

Sam's attitude was to keep the beach well policed, develop a dialogue with the bathers on his beach, and develop a cooperative relationship. He saw his job as one of educating bathers of the water hazards and the reasons for restrictions. He took a proactive approach and avoided ignoring small problems before they became big ones. He taught me to walk along the beach and talk to people rather than toot on the whistle all the time. We worked well together, and as the season went on, he drew me into his confidence more and more.

Sam taught me to avoid the temptation of looking for more than a few seconds at people I was talking to and to always face the water. He helped to condition me to get used to scanning the water and the beach regularly.

He got me to loosen up a bit and not do everything "by the book" when it did not seem to count—like waiting until he had gotten to his car before "calling him out" for lunch. (When we left the beach for lunch or head breaks, we were supposed to call the shack on the phone to report we were leaving the beach. Since we were only supposed to take a half hour for lunch, and it sometimes took a while to find a parking space, we would try to sneak a few extra minutes by having our partner call us out after we had a few minutes head start.) Years later, referring to his slow, ambling gait, and tendency to stop and visit with people along his path, Sam would tell me, "Back then, I was really slow on land."

Sam ran such a good beach, and we had so few bad water days, that I did not have a rescue my entire first year. Of course I wanted one, just so I wouldn't be a "cherry," but that went away the next year when we had a stream of rough water days.

Viking Attack

GORDON H. - It must have been within the first few days on the job that Sam suggested we take the surfboat out together. My weeks of practicing with Andy had prepared me with the rowing skills, but not the combat we were about to encounter. Roger and Andy came up from the next beach in their boat, taunting, splashing, and jeering, and tried to ram us. We held them off with our oars, but in the ensuing confusion, someone grabbed an oar belonging to the other boat, and they were, in effect, "crippled," like a four-cylinder engine that was running on three cylinders. After more taunts and jeers, the purloined oar was tossed into the water for the losers to retrieve.

The Boat

MICKEY H. - There were two types of boats used on the Jersey Shore when I guarded in the '60s and '70s. The wood Hankins and the fiberglass Van Dynes. Since I guarded at several beaches, I was able to experience both types. The fiberglass boats were a little lighter and faster to row, but the Hankins rode waves better. Since I was into riding waves, I liked the Hankins the best.

I probably spent more time in a Hankins than most of the other guards. Rowing a Hankins was a great workout. It was really enjoyable to punch through waves and feel the momentum build up as you rowed. It was nice to be able to row out into the ocean to get away from the noise and confusion on the beach. It gave you a real sense of freedom. I always thought of the boats as one of the "perks" for guarding on the beach.

Guard boats were an historic tradition, kind of like the U.S. Cavalry's horses and swords. Almost every guard uniform had a picture of a boat or crossed oars somewhere on it. In the ten summers I guarded, I only saw a few boat rescues. Once one of my partners was rowing back from a workout when we saw him stop and pick up a girl that was out a ways. We thought that he was trying to make the moves on her, but he said that she looked tired when he went by; he asked her if she wanted a ride, and she said yes.

Probably the most common type of boat rescue occurred when someone got blown out to sea on a raft during a day with a strong offshore wind. You could just row out, load them in the boat, and haul them onto the beach. It was generally easier to do it this way than to try to swim them in or paddle them in on a rescue board.

On the whole, I always felt that the boats were too bulky for most of the rescues that we had to make, especially on a rough day. You could almost always get to someone in trouble faster on a rescue board then you could in a boat. Besides, rowing an eight hundred-pound boat through a bunch of swimmers to get to someone in a rip was asking for trouble. If you missed a stroke, you could bash their head in with an oar. If a freak wave hit you, and you lost control in a swimming area, you could take out a lot of swimmers with a heavy Hankins.

Beer Fishing

GORDON H. - The next time we went out in the boat, the party boats (boats loaded with tourist fisherman) were in close to the beach—only a few hundred yards offshore. Sam and I rowed out to the seaward side of the fishing boat and out of sight of watchful eyes on the shoreline. Sam struck up a quick conversation with the fishermen.

"How's the fishin' today?" he yelled amicably. The men lining the deck rail all shrugged their shoulders. No one had caught anything yet.

"What kind of bait are you using?" he pressed with what I began to suspect was false interest.

"Jigs," replied one of the fishermen. "The guys on the other side are using mullet."

"Oh," Sam replied, the topic exhausted. "You guys got a beer you could spare?"

Several men on the boat broke into smiles. One reached into his cooler and flipped one to Sam.

"Good luck," Sam replied as he began to dip and pull the oars. "I hope you catch some big ones."

The Happy Blue Boat

KENNY J. ('67-'69) - My stand buddy in Bay Head was Danny. He had some friends who had a blue boat that would come out right in front of our area. He would swim out to it, get on the boat, stay for five minutes, and come back. While he was there he would smoke a joint. He'd say, "Here comes the Happy Blue Boat, I gotta go out."

Perks And Peaks

GORDON H. - One week, there was this teenage girl who kept hanging around the stand and wanting our attention. She was probably seventeen or eighteen and had a very nice figure in a pretty two-piece that, from our vantage point, was very eye-catching. She seemed to be dying for our attention. Sam and I played along with her for a day or two. Then one day she started digging in the sand right in front of the stand, and the top to her suit popped open. For less than a second, she was revealed, but it was long enough to jolt us out of the doldrums.

"Oooh! Nice bubbies," was Sam's reaction. "Why don't you do

that again?"

First Rescue

BOB G. - I was all alone for my first pull. Archie M. was out for lunch or on a break. Billy Newman, an ex-guard, helped out. Years later, we had about thirty rescues in one day, but most of them were little ones.

Head Break Shyness

GORDON H. - When the regular dispatcher for the beach patrol took a day off, sometimes one of the women that normally guarded at the bay beaches would handle the switchboard at headquarters. There was a no-frills bathroom there with a paper-thin partition. Guards would often borrow a bike and pedal on the boardwalk to take "head breaks" at the guard shack.

After one trip, Andy's partner, Duke, accused him of being timid about urinating when a woman was in the guard shack.

"Andy," he said, "you're the kind of guy who goes to his girl-friend's house and puts his foot in the toilet and lets it run down his leg so it won't make any noise."

Rookie In The Fog

MICKEY H. - The last year I was guarding in Lavallette, Roy and I took out one of the rookies to do some wave riding on a foggy June afternoon. The rookie was a little spooked about boating since he had been hit on the head with an oar during a Viking war the previous week. However, we were able to talk him into it. We spent quite a bit of time getting him used to rowing and feeling comfortable in the boat before we decided to ride some waves. Unfortunately, the fog got so thick when we were out there that we could not see the beach.

We finally got close enough in so that we could go for a wave. The rookie was in the bow seat, Roy was rowing in the second seat, and I was steering in the back. It took us a while to try to get lined up because it was a pretty good-sized swell and a high tide, so the jetties were almost completely covered with water and difficult to spot. We had to pull out at the last minute on the first wave that we tried to take because we were headed directly for a partially submerged jetty. The rookie was getting pretty freaked out by now, but we said it was no big deal, and we could still catch a wave in.

We finally lined up a good-sized wave and dropped in. Everything went fine as we went across the bar, then it backed off just a little before it turned into a five-foot shorebreak, dropping onto dry sand. Roy and I could see what was coming and yelled for the rookie to bail out as we flipped over the back of the boat. Getting tangled up in a Hankins on a big wave in shallow water is highly undesirable. Unfortunately, the rookie froze in his seat. By some miracle, the Hankins hit the beach with him in it, rolled back and forth, but did not flip over on top of him. He was white, and his eyes were like saucers when we got to the beach. We practically had to pry him out of the boat. We also found out that we were about two beaches south of where we started. We had to leave the boat at that beach and walk back to our beach because the fog was so thick. We were never able to get that rookie back into a boat.

Breaking In Rookies

GORDON H. - I guarded for nearly three years before I was assigned a rookie to break in. His name was Rusty. He was a big fellow with a strong streak of vanity. I think he was used to getting a lot of attention as a big shot high school football player. He was a fairly good student of lifeguarding, but did little to alleviate the tedium of the watch.

The following year, I was assigned Roy. Roy was from the Boston area and, because of his speech mannerisms, first reminded me of Mortimer Snerd, ventriloquist Edgar Bergen's dummy. He had blazing reddish-blond hair, a rough complexion, and blue eyes. He had a small frame and a lax attitude. He rarely asked questions, and I continually had to remind him, particularly when he was talking to a girl, to face the ocean.

He turned out to be a good guard, but I never felt confident about his powers of observation. One of my biggest scares came late one afternoon after working a part time job that kept me up until 2:00 a.m. the previous night. I began to get dulled over from lack of sleep. I glanced to my side and saw that he was falling asleep as well. That gave me a jolt of adrenaline. From that point on, I was wide-awake.

Staying Dry

DAVE M. (late '60s, '74) - The only advice I ever remember getting from another guard was when we were watching some swimmers getting close to the rip.

"Do you see those people there?" he asked.

I said, "Yes."

"Do you realize that in a few moments they will be in trouble and need to be rescued? Why don't you go over and get them away from the undertow before we have to rescue them."

When I returned to the stand after moving the people over, my partner said, "Remember, a dry guard is a good guard."

Something Stupid

SAM H. - Talk about pranks and everything. As a rookie, Andy always used to wear a Monmouth College sweatshirt, and Roger used to put tape over the "Mon" and make it Mouth College. He'd make Andy wear it. Roger used to always bust his balls.

Mopsic's Sister

SAM H. - Mopsick and Dick H. were sitting on the stand. Dick could bust people's balls pretty good. So Ron's fat sister walks up and talks to Mopsick for a while. Dick doesn't know it's his sister. When she jumps in the water, Dick said, "Whooooa, where'd you meet that one?! You can do a lot better than that." And he went on and on and on—just ragging him about this hefty woman. I mean he just killed her. And finally Mopsick said, "That's my sister."

Pete

GORDON H. - I met Pete the first day I worked with him at the Surf Club. It was a three-man beach, with one of the three men being Jim D., the asshole captain. Our morning routine was to clean the litter off the three hundred-foot long beach, set up the equipment, and then have breakfast at the Club's snack bar. On this Saturday, Jim D. was bitching how Pete was ten minutes late for work, and he was going to get fired if he did this again. At this moment Pete arrived. A Marlboro dangled from his lips. He wore "too cool" wrap-around sunglasses. He had dark Italian features, a stocky build, and carried a gym bag. The conversation went like this.

Jim D.: "You're late Locascio!"

Pete: "Well, I got laid last night."

Jim D. was stunned by the irrefutable argument implicit in the statement, but continued anyway.

Jim D. "You'll get fired if you're late again."

Pete: "I'll try not to do it again."

Jim D.: "Now help us clean up the beach."

Pete looked over to me, lifted up his glasses, and gave me a look that said, "Is this asshole for real?" Clearly, Pete did not consider garbage detail part of his lifeguard job description.

I walked over, introduced myself, and we shook hands. Then we began to pick up the litter on the beach, mostly cups and glasses from the bar and snack bar. Actually, Jim D. and I picked up the litter—Pete walked along slightly to the side and behind Jim D. With his foot, Pete would push the litter under the soft sand. When he saw me notice this—and smile at his outlandishness and defiance—he began to strike ballet poses each time he shoved the scraps of paper products under the sand.

Pete was a law student earning his way through college by working at a welfare agency. He came to the shore on weekends and guarded on our three-man beach as the relief man. Bright, witty, and arrogant, he prided himself on being a great seducer. Guarding with him was always entertaining—he had great tales to tell and his observations were always acute, and usually sarcastic. He loved to "goof" on people, leaving them slightly off-balance.

Throughout the day on the beach, people would regularly come up and ask us questions, things like the time or information about the tides. Why they asked us for the time always puzzled me. Usually it was clear that we weren't wearing watches, and often all we had on was a pair of trunks, a whistle, and sunglasses.

When Pete was first asked the time, the conversation went like this.

Bather: "What time is it?"

Pete: "The-mome-raths-outgrabe."

Bather: "What?"

Pete (slowly, clearly annunciated, and slightly annoyed): "THE-MOME-RATHS-OUTGRABE."

Bather (just before walking away totally befuddled): "Oh. Thanks."

A Guard That Froze

JOE S. ('68-'76, '90s, '00s) - Tom L. didn't last long. He worked as a guard, and one day, we had a cardiac arrest. A woman ran over to tell him. Tom froze on the stand—he got scared. He was a very nice kid. The captain told him he had to help out. Then we had a couple of pulls. I was the rope guy—I swam out and made it to the people. He never left the stand.

Another time, Tom was in the water on a rescue, and he was floundering. I was out there already with five people. It wasn't a serious rescue: we were just caught in a run, and we had them under control. He couldn't get himself to the people 'cause he was scared. Some of the old guards—John M., Russ F.—grabbed the can from him and helped with the rescue. Tom's parents were on the beach and came over to me afterward and said, "You don't want him to be your partner, do you?" At that point, I said, "No."

He was a nice kid, but he was eighteen and immature.

Why Joe Was A Good Guard

JIMMY A. - Joe S. was a good guard. We got along really good. We sat together two years. He was the best straight man: he would lie for you with a straight face.

Discourse On Women Lifeguarding

BOBBI A. ('65-'69) - I wanted to go up to the ocean and guard. At the end of the season, when they were short on guards and beach cops, I went up to the ocean and worked as a beach cop/third guard. I was there as a backup for the regular guards, maybe less than a week. I don't think I was allowed to sit on the stand.

GORDON H. - It's interesting to see the evolution of women working as guards. First, they got jobs on the bay that nobody wanted. Then, they worked occasionally as beach cops and emergency guards. And now, they work on the ocean fulltime.

JIMMY A. - It was like everything else with women. They get a foothold in one tiny crease, and then they all try to rush through it.

On Women Lifeguards

DICK H. - The first women began on the ocean in 1976 when a councilwoman was in charge of the beach. I had no problem with the woman—she had to do everything the guys had to do. That was part of the test. See, the guys didn't have to move the lifeguard stand, but the women had to. And they had to move a boat.

On Being One Of The First Women Ocean Lifeguards

MICHELLE P. ('77-'80, '83-'84) - It was not easy for me, as a female lifeguard on the Atlantic Ocean.

I lifeguarded '77 to '80 and '83 in Lavallette. My first year was on the bay. Actually, I started that summer in the salt-water pool at Casino Pier in the Heights. After one "real" rescue, drug searches in the locker rooms, and having to break up a couple having sex under a lawn chair, I decided to try out as a bay guard in Lavallette. I easily got the bay job, but wasn't too challenged nor stimulated by the position.

The next summer ('78), another woman was trying out for a beach lifeguard slot. I knew from the previous summer that I could beat most of the guys in the water. I was both a competitive pool swimmer and an ocean swimmer. Lifeguarding on the beach certainly appeared more exciting than the bay. So I went for it.

I remember that the water was fifty-eight degrees. Guys were coming out of the swim test sucking air and puking. I not only swam faster, but also could hold a conversation afterwards. While my swim time was admirable, Dick, the captain, called me into the shack later and explained that women belonged on the bay. He "needed" me on the bay. I don't remember exactly what words were spoken, but I remember walking out of the shack wondering if I had a job. He had only spoken of the bay; I had only spoken of the ocean. So, I simply showed up for the first day of work. He somehow acknowledged that I was on a trial basis. My trial never ended.

Dick did not know what to do with Karen, the other female ocean guard, nor myself. He made us permanent rovers. For the entire season.

Being a rover is somewhat lonely. You never really get to know any other guards well. Most guards were somewhat uncomfortable sitting with a female. Being young and having an abundance of testosterone, they were unsure what to do when a female was beside them. Can't talk about the "babes." Can't talk about last night's "conquest." Can't talk about the Phillies. So mostly I remember long days listening to the radio.

Dick had favorites to sit me with—the bigger guys, like Sweeney, and placed me mostly at the north end where it was calmer. I felt like everyday I had to prove that I was at least equal to the male guards. Every morning during the workout, I swam harder, ran faster, did more push ups or sit-ups, or whatever it took to prove that I was competent.

I am not a militant feminist. I was young and merely wanted to do a job that I knew that I could do well, but never felt that anyone believed me.

Because I was a strong swimmer, I used to be in the tournaments. Swim relay, rope pull...that always created a stir. Some local paper ran an article once. I don't have a copy, but I remember feeling proud to be acknowledged. The guys I swam against usually held a grudge. When we would get together afterwards, few would say "great race—you really gave me a run for my money." Instead, they took it as an insult that they were in competition with a *girl*.

My second year, "Cosmic" George T. agreed to sit with me. As I was no longer officially a rookie, he did not have the license to do terrible hazing types of things. He did some pranks anyway, like dumping me off the stand by tipping it forward, running me off the boardwalk on our bikes, and instructing me to lift the anchors when it didn't need to be done. But George did teach me more about guarding. He taught me how to watch the ocean and the people in it. He also expounded on his philosophies of life and love.

Sam was our beach cop. A New York City guy. He was tough and sensitive. He rounded out our peculiar beach. Never was there a more unique threesome. I looked forward to each day.

The following year, I was assigned a rookie, Bill G. He hated that his senior partner was a female. And he let me know it. He was a serious guard, and he considered me a bad twist of fate. In the end, however, he became one of the best guards and went on to become a lieutenant in Lavallette.

In '83, I returned, after I went back to school to get my Masters. By then, Cres was the captain, and much had changed. I felt much more accepted. But I also felt too old. The glamour was gone. The "All Female" tournament had been initiated. Women were on the beach to stay. Those parts seemed easier. Now the odd part was my age. Again, partners had little to discuss with me. The age limit had been decreased to seventeen, and I was a twenty-five-year old female. I had little in common with many bench partners. I think I spent that year as a rover as well.

So, that is a summary of my summers as a lifeguard. In some ways, it was difficult. But mostly I loved the job. I love the ocean. I love the beach. Getting paid to sit and watch the waves is my idea of a great deal. The ocean is soothing, majestic, not to be overruled. Storms are great. Sunny days are delightful.

Why Women Watch The Water Better

JACK C. ('77-present) - Sometimes women are the best people to sit with. They watch the water because they know their limited physical strength. They watch the water much better and don't have the ego problems of the guys. The down side is dragging the stands down to the water for them.

The Anatomy Of A Water Killer

GORDON H. - Most rescues don't just happen, they develop. Guards learn to look for the telltale signs of a belabored swimmer: head low in the water, arm strokes barely clearing the surface, a body caught in the current offering resistance to no avail, the "ugly look"— then you know it's time to rescue. But most rescues in our area are the result of a seapuss, also known as a rip current or an undertow. The term seapuss seems to be regional, perhaps confined to New Jersey.

Whatever it is called, it is a the product of simple hydrodynamics: waves bring in thousands of gallons of water over a sandbar, the water seeks its own level and drains through the deepest channel—a low spot along the edge of the sandbar. The run can be mild or vicious. An experienced ocean swimmer learns to use the run to his advantage: hop in it to get out to catch waves or reach someone beyond the sandbar. To the unwary and uninformed, it can be fatal.

Most often, victims are washed across the sandbar after a heavy set of waves has brought massive amounts of water to the beach. This raises the water level so that bathers, who a few moments before were standing in knee-deep water, find themselves up to their chests in a swiftly moving current. The current rarely alarms the bathers until they drift into the seapuss and discover that their feet cannot reach the bottom. It is then that they begin to wash away from the shore. They usually struggle to swim in to the beach, get exhausted, and then they are seized by panic.

To get out of the seapuss, all the swimmer would have to do is swim to the side of the undertow's current, and he or she would find themselves in calmer and less treacherous water. Rarely is a seapuss more than ten yards wide and usually it dissipates after thirty or forty yards. They are easy to spot on the incoming tide by the rippled surface water moving away from the shoreline. Often the water in the run has suspended sediment moving out to sea in a mushroom-shaped plume. Occasionally, the run will move across the beach as the sand in the sandbar shifts with the current.

A guard carries a torpedo buoy during a rescue drill, keeping his eye on the "victim" the whole time. As guards get older, many seem to feel the jolt of the cold water temperatures more, which can drop as low as fifty degrees when west winds blow the warm surface water out to sea.

July
Into The Breach

By July, bench partners have begun to become accustomed to one another. They develop a style of guarding established by the senior partner. Rookie and junior partners are quickly apprised of the "pecking order" and learn the appropriate subservience to the veterans' wisdom or priorities. Under the best of circumstances, the bench partners complement each other's style.

Water temperatures tend to be more stable in July, although west winds can make the temperatures plummet into the forties when the warm surface water is pushed out to sea and the cold bottom water takes its place. Although the sandbars constantly shift their sands, they seem more stable in July than at any other time.

The mornings may involve drills or the guards may be dispatched directly to their beach. Once there, they set up the gear. If they are diligent, they may even exercise. The stands are dragged down close to the water. The line boxes and buoys are carried down to the base of the stand. The boats are rolled down from their overturned berths near the dunes and boardwalks.

If there is time, the guards might practice rowing together in the boat. More often than not, they are shaking the cobwebs out of their heads from the previous late night outing and passing on guy gossip. Sometimes a simple head soak begins to get the blood flowing through brains and bodies addled by beer and other concoctions. Partners learn about each other's families, colleges, girlfriends, and fiancées. Confidences flow.

If they do take out the boats, often they will meet with neighboring beaches offshore and have "Viking wars" that consist mostly of spitting contests and trying to short-oar each other's boat.

Most beaches tend to have a relaxed atmosphere until the Fourth of July weekend. Then it seems as if everyone on the beach was just released from a mental institution with no sense of self-preservation. Like lemmings they appear, drawn by mystical forces. Overheated macho guys will race headlong into the ocean only to discover it is only fifteen degrees above freezing. Adults and children alike will scamper across grease-slick, seaweed-covered jetty boulders, oblivious to the potential of horrible consequences. People with perfectly white skin will spend the entire day under the blazing sun with no protection, anxious to get a jump-start on their summer tan. Some guards develop a distain for tourists—and sometimes, for reasons that are subject to debate, they are called "bennies."

If the guards are lucky, the water will be calm. If not, they may be on their feet for most of the day. Seasoned guards and well-tutored rookies will walk along the beach, talking to bathers and explaining the reasons for restricted areas. It is an effective time investment that develops better rapport with the beach crowd and avoids the annoyance of whistles being blown every two minutes.

♠ ♠ ♠

Hoopies

JIMMY A. ('66-'67) - Hoopies! They were hoopies. (The people that were ignorant of the water and would not listen to the guards.)

The Rush

MICKEY H. ('67-'76) - Most summers, you would sit on the bench for days at a time being bored and watching the hours drag by. I remember some summers where I did not make more than one or two minor rescues. However, when you did see someone in trouble, and knew you had to go after them, it was a real adrenalin rush. I remember making some wild jumps over waves and some incredible sprints through the surf to get to the people. There were more than a few times where I remember being wet all day from one rescue to another. Those days went really fast. You hardly had time to look at your watch before it was time to close down the beach.

Sharks!

MICKEY H. - Sharks were the boogieman of the Jersey coast. It was every tourist's nightmare to be attacked by a shark or to even see a shark. In reality, they had a much greater chance of being killed walking from their cottage to the beach in the morning.

Every summer, we always had at least several shark scares. The lifeguards would stand up on their bench, blow the whistles, and get everyone out of the water. It was strange to look up and down the beach and see an empty ocean with everyone standing on the beach looking out at the water. After an hour or so, the guards would slowly let the people back in. Usually in a few hours, everything was back to normal.

I guess there was some reason for the ceremony since, once when I was really young, a shark did attack a wader in waist-deep water in Sea Girt and took off his leg. In the early part of the century, a single shark attacked and killed about four people in a one-week period along the Jersey Shore. That may have helped Peter Benchley get the idea for

Jaws. Over the years, I have visited a number of sea life parks that have shark tanks. The thing that I always noticed is that, most of the time, the sharks did not cruise along the surface with their dorsal fins sticking out of the water. More often than not, they were cruising along the bottom. Taking that into consideration, I figured that for every shark that was ever spotted off the beach, there probably were another ten that were quietly cruising along the bottom checking out the tourists' legs.

After a while, I did not put much faith in shark scares. Up to that point, I never saw one or actually met another guard that really did have a confirmed shark sighting. It was always the next town down or the beach to the north that saw the "shark." I even knew some guards to fake a shark scare because they had a bad hangover and did not want to have to watch the water. A couple of times, I actually swam out to get a kid's beach ball or surf mat during a shark scare if they lost it in their panic to leave the water. I felt it gave the tourists a good story to tell when they got home. I was used to the possibility of sharks being around since I had been doing a lot of surfing in the tropical waters of Mexico and Central America in the winter where there was a real possibility of an encounter.

Once they had a shark scare when I was working at Island Beach State Park, just three miles south of Lavallette. After calling in all the swimmers, some of the guards went out in the guard boats to look for the shark. I figured it was another bogus scare, so I paddled out on a surfboard to look. When I was about seventy-five yards out, I saw a large fin pass between me and the nearest guard boat that was only one hundred feet away. The guards in the boat said it was an eight-foot hammerhead. I made really shallow strokes as I paddled the board back to the beach.

Seapuss Attack

GORDON H. ('65-'73, '75) - Sometimes people on the beach

resented the lifeguards. They started out with the anti-authority preju-
dice that you were a punk, a jock, or a cop. One Saturday, there was a
father and three kids wading not far from the jetty. The water was calm,
but because I wanted to establish the boundaries of the bathing area
(and did not want to start a trend where everyone started bathing wherever they felt like it), I whistled, pointed at them when they looked up,
and then pointed to the bathing area which was lined with buoys. With
his left hand on the inside of his right elbow, the guy raised his fist with
a bent elbow in the universal sign language for "Fuck You!"

Now when I was younger, I would have gotten more upset, but I
had been working on the beach for two or three years and decided to
take a diplomatic approach. I walked over to the family, watching the
father beginning to brace for a confrontation. He looked like he was
aching for an argument.

As I got closer, I very calmly said, "Sir, your children are bathing
right next to a seapuss, and they would be safer in the marked bathing
area."

The father jolted: *"Seapuss?!* Come on kids, get out of the water!"

He dashed in with his arms outstretched to his children, whom he
must have expected to be devoured by a ferocious creature at any
moment. He never asked what a seapuss was, and he never gave me any
more problems.

July 4, 1972

MICKEY H. - One of the best parties I remember was on the
Fourth of July, 1972. Most of my friends agree that, for some reason,
1972 was the best for parties and wild women. Anyway, on that Fourth,
I held a guard party on my family's beach in Ortley. At that time, my
family owned a fifty-foot stretch of beach just north of the Surf Club.
They had a five-unit apartment building on it called the Golden Gull
and lived on the third floor with the best view in town.

Since it was a private beach, we did not have to worry about being bothered by the police, even though there were quite a few underage people drinking at the party. It started off as a typical hunch-punch party along with a keg or two. My family had an old cannon. (It was a miniature version of the type of cannons that you see on old pirate ships.) It was about three feet long and three feet high, weighing about one hundred pounds. I am not sure how we came into possession of the cannon. My parents would never really explain it to me. I have a feeling that it may have had something to do with a wild lifeguard party back in the 1940s.

One of my sister's boyfriends had a knack for making homemade explosives. Every half hour he would fill the cannon with explosives, wad it down with newspaper, and fire it off. One of my friends was taking a leak down by the ocean and got covered with powder and shredded wadding when they set it off behind him.

About half way through the party I met this extremely well-endowed young lady. Periodically, we would leave the party for my room. By midnight, everyone was either passed out or had found someone to take home, and things quieted down.

The next morning, it was rainy and there was a blue mood when I arrived at the guard shack. Two of the guards had left the party with some young ladies and taken them to their house for a more intimate party. From what I heard, the girls were not overly cooperative and one of the guards who was quite drunk lost interest and started lighting and throwing cherry bombs out the window of the house. Unbeknownst to them, they lived next door to the Lavallette police chief. When they got in their car to drive the girls home, they were immediately pulled over by the police. As well as being drunk, they had some grass in the car. They might have gotten away with being drunk and loud, but the grass was the straw that broke the camel's back. They both got busted and kicked off the guard squad. It was even worse, because one of them was a teacher, and he also lost his full-time teaching job.

Best Boat Wipeout

MICKEY H. - Ken C. and I were out in early July when the water was still pretty cold. He was in the back seat, and I was in the front. We made a really late takeoff on a six-foot wave. He jumped to the back of the boat to steer as we started to drop in. The drop was so steep that I was thrown out of my seat and into the bottom of the boat. I remember looking up at the sky and then looking at water rushing up at me. The bow of the boat pearled and then flipped completely upside down. Ken was thrown through the air, and I was inside the boat underwater. The guards on the beach said it looked like *The Wide World of Sports*. It took a lot of effort to get the boat in, and we just missed washing up on a jetty.

Oversight

ARCHIE M. ('58-'64) - Charlie used to get a twitch in his toe when something was going to happen. I was sitting on the stand one day when the water was really calm, and he went to lunch. And all of a sudden, the people on the beach started pointing and screaming, pointing and screaming. All I could see was someone's back. They were floating face down. The water was as calm as it could be. So I jumped in the water. By the time I got out there, I was half-exhausted. When I got this guy in—he was a young fellow—he was crouched over in a fetal position and stiff as a board. I couldn't get a can under him— it was terrible. I got him to the edge of the water, and finally some people came down and helped me drag him up on the beach. Dick Ginglen was my beach cop that day. I was giving him artificial respiration (back pressure, arm lift method). It took a long time; he was out for the duration. I worked on him until the ambulance got there. Finally, with the artificial respiration, he started vomiting, and he came around (but he spent the next three days in the hospital). With all this going on, Charlie was sitting at home having lunch with his twitching toe when he heard the first aid whistle go off. He just left and knew exactly where to go and what was happening. I'll never forget that day. And it took me a while to recuperate—I just took the rest of the day off. Every fiber in my body was twitching from the nerves. That was a very close call.

We don't know what caused it. I don't think I ever saw him again. His parents came up and thanked me and everything, but that was about it.

Vacancy Outside

GORDON H. - Sometimes the people on the beach would amaze you. It was like they forgot to pack their brains when they went on vacation. I watched people on the beach sit in their beach chairs, book on their lap, watching the tide come in and the waves getting closer and closer. They'd even watch other people's towels and beach paraphernalia get sopped, never considering it could happen to their valuables. Finally a monster wave would come up and soak everything—towels, radios, cameras, chairs, and other stuff. They would react in slow motion, as if they hadn't had nearly an hour's warning that the tide was coming up on the beach.

The Horror

RUSSELL F. ('50-'51) - Back then, they had the ropes attached to the pilings to mark the bathing areas, and the people would go out and hold onto the ropes. The biggest pulls we had in those days were the old ladies who were holding onto the ropes and losing their bathing suits. We had to pull up their bathing suits before we helped to bring them in—they were big, fat, old ladies. Boy, was that embarrassing.

First Day On The Beach

JACK C. ('77-present) - I remember my first day in Lavallette. I had more pulls my first day than I had my whole year at Midway. We were just plucking them out.

Tangled Up In Blue

TOM A. ('63-'70) - Every beach on the Jersey Shore was closed. It was July, and there was a storm. For some reason, the Bay Head Improvement Association (known as the BHIA) decided not to close the beaches in Bay Head. So, people decided to go out and be heroes. They got caught—it was at least a half dozen—and we had to go out. I happened to be the one lucky enough to go out with the line. Three cans had gone out already, and I had everyone on the cans to bring in. People on the beach, in their desire to help, started yanking the line as hard as they could before I could get the belt up around my chest. Then, we get in this gigantic surf. I get pulled under. A wave comes in. It just separates me. I get turned around. The next thing I know, I got all kinds of lines twisted on me, and I can't swim, and I'm underwater. If it hadn't been for my friend, Jack McGuinity, and his brother, I could have been a goner. They happened to be on the beach and watching. They ran out and stopped them from pulling. When I got to shore, I wasn't unconscious, but I was full of water.

P.S. They closed the beach after that. A light went up on the street—do you understand what I'm saying?

Spears With Sails

GORDON H. - Perhaps there is no greater danger on the beach than umbrellas. Often people will leave them on the beach while they go home for lunch. The wind invariably gains intensity after 2:00 p.m., and the beachgoers' shade devices, often left unattended, become erratically-spiraling pointed missiles. The greatest danger I saw in my years of guarding was when a slim-poled, blue-striped umbrella went flying end over end with the wind. By the time I rocketed off the stand to try to stop it, it had stuck deeply into the sand just inches from an infant's heart. Time and again, I saw umbrellas lifted into the air and careen down the beach, threatening anything in their path.

West Wind Peril

GORDON H. - A west wind can be even more deadly, particularly when two or more people climb on the same raft. The danger is even greater when the raft is made of light plastic. Before the rafters are aware of it, the wind blows them outside of the designated area.

Visions Of Mortality

GORDON H. - When I was a youngster, one of my sisters rented out beach chairs, umbrellas, and rafts at the beach in Seaside Park. One day, two children, perhaps not quite teenagers, had been blown away from the shore on a light plastic raft by a strong west wind. The guards kept whistling at them to come back into the beach area. Lying across the length of the raft, they paddled hard but inefficiently, causing more splashing than movement. They began to get scared and panicked. Without warning, they decided to abandon their raft and swim to shore. The raft quickly spun away in the strong gusts. By then, they were nearly exhausted and their condition quickly became perilous. The guards jumped into the water, but could not get to them before the kids went under. They were lost—drowned.

Anytime I felt myself getting cocky as a lifeguard, I recalled the sick, sad feeling I had that day years earlier knowing that those lives had come to spend an innocent day at the beach, and it had gone terribly awry.

Bay Beach Hazards And Perks

PATRICIA D. ('67-'69) - I *sort of* had pulls. It would usually come from kids jumping off the dock at one corner where it was deep. Another time, a kid flipped a tube and got caught in it upside down. I'd just have to get them turned over. It was nothing serious; they just had their feet up in the air.

I had more problems with parents saying that it was too shallow and going out too far. They would ignore the whistle and walk out toward the channel. They'd say, "I'm an adult, and you can't tell me what to do." I had to explain that there are boats, that they are bigger than you, and they have the right of way.

The kids would all bring me fruit. There was always a group of kids.

The Impact Of The Movie *Jaws*

MICKEY H. - This movie probably had more impact on tourists than any other movie that ever came out. It came to the local theaters in July, and by the end of the month, you could see the difference. Now there has been so much exposure to it—and so many sequels—that it doesn't have the same impact, but it sure was intense when it first came out.

The movie theater was packed, and the girl I took was several years older than myself and a long-time friend of one of my sisters. It was the first time that we had ever really gone out. Hell, parts of the movie were so scary that some little kid sitting next to us would grab the girl I was with, he was so scared. The images and sound effects were so intense that she was crawling all over me in the first ten minutes. Of course, I was glad to do whatever I could to help comfort her, which turned into an all night event in my bed.

That summer, we did not have many problems with swimmers going out too far. I had a set of shark jaws from a ten-foot shark that I got in Mexico. They were really nasty looking. I use to hang them behind my bench. The tourists really used to freak out when they saw them, and I told them that is what the business end of a shark looked like. Every time I went swimming that summer, I could hear the music from *Jaws* when I got into deep water. Sometimes I wish they had never made that movie. To me, that movie was scarier than any monster movie ever made because the monster was real and almost everything that occurred in that movie—except the ending—had occurred in real life at one time or another.

Ocean Sunfish

MICKEY H. - Ocean sunfish are one of the strangest looking fish in the sea. They basically consist of a giant head with big dorsal and ventral fins. They often slowly swim along the surface with just the dorsal fin sticking out of the water. Until you get real close, it looks like a big shark fin. They are basically a warm water fish, and I did not see them very often.

In 1975, I was sitting on the bench on a glassy, warm afternoon when I saw a large fin off the beach. We immediately got everyone out of the water, and we jumped into the guard boat to check it out. As usual, we felt invincible in our trusty Hankins.

When we finally got out there, we realized it was only a harmless ocean sunfish. I always felt that at least a small part of our job was entertaining the tourists, since the most exciting trip many of them had ever been on was a two-week vacation at the Jersey Shore. I thought that they might be disappointed if we got back to the beach and told them it was only a harmless sunfish. So, I stood on the back of the boat and made like I was beating a dangerous shark with an oar. Dwayne and I were hollering and yelling and making a real ruckus. Then I "accidentally" fell overboard and landed on top of the "shark" and made like we were fighting it out. We were over one hundred yards out, but we could hear the people screaming on the beach. They thought that they were watching a lifeguard getting eaten by a shark. After wrestling with the sunfish for a few minutes, he got tired and headed for the bottom. My chest and stomach were a little scratched up from wrestling the sunfish, so there was dramatic effect from the blood trickling down my side when we got to the beach. The tourists had all kinds of questions as we landed the boat, but we just kind of mumbled answers and let them make their own conclusions.

Cave-in

TOM A. - A mother comes running up to the stand, "My baby! My baby!" Right away, your first reaction is to look in the water. Nothing! Everybody was standing on one side of the beach. Apparently, they had dug a big hole down about two feet. The next thing you knew, the whole thing had collapsed. She had a one or two-year old child. We had to dig down at least two feet with our bare hands. When we got to the baby, it was almost blue. I think it was the only time I did mouth-to-mouth in all my time guarding. Afterward, our fingers were bleeding. You don't realize it at the time, but that sand was like sandpaper and tore up our hands in our frantic digging to get to the baby.

Lost Kids

MICKEY H. - Little kids were always getting lost at the beach. It was easy to see why: they are short with a restricted view on a flat beach and at an unfamiliar, crowded place. They would be playing at the water's edge and then decide to walk back to their parent's blanket. If they made the slightest miscalculation, they would end up lost in a sea of blankets, umbrellas, beach chairs, and strangers. What happened next would depend on the wind. If there was a wind blowing, they would almost always start looking for their family with the wind at their back. Little kids hate to walk into a strong wind. Since most afternoons we had a strong southeast wind, the kids usually walked to the north.

Even knowing this, you still got a slight rush when a mother came running up to the stand with her eyes bugging out shouting, "My little boy was playing at the water's edge, and he is gone, please help me. Do something—you are a lifeguard!"

We had to calm them down and tell them to start looking to the north. The kids would always show up; it just took a little longer some days. One Labor Day, a kid got lost on a beach that Ken C. was guarding, and they did not find the kid until 7:00 p.m. that night. Another time, Bruce sent a twenty-one-year old guy with Downs Syndrome to the next lifeguard bench to get some "shoreline." Before he got there, he forgot what he was looking for and got lost. Bruce did not always use the best judgment and got in a lot of trouble for that one.

When I found a lost kid, we would bring the kid up on the bench with us and get him calmed down. Then we would have a "kid auction." My partner would hold up the kid while I blew my whistle as loud as I could and asked for bids. Nine times out of ten the parents would see their kid and come running before we got any offers.

Passed Out

MICKEY H. - In 1974, I was sitting on the bench watching the crowd and checking out this one, well-built young woman standing in waist-deep water. All of a sudden she started to weave and bob. The next thing I knew, she just fell over into the water. I ran as fast as I could, but she was under water by the time I got to her. I immediately picked her up and signaled for one of my partners to call for an ambulance.

Her sister saw me carrying her up the beach and said, "She has done it again." I gave her some smelling salts, and she woke up bitchy as hell. I told her that an ambulance was on the way, but she did not want any part of it. Her sister told me that it was no big deal, that she did this all of the time. It turned out that she had a brain tumor that occasionally caused her to just pass out.

She told me that her brother had the same condition and had drowned at a nearby beach when he was out swimming in a crowd and the lifeguards did not see him pass out and go under. This was great: a hardheaded woman that went wading by herself and could pass out without warning at any second. That week was really stressful watching her every moment as well as the rest of the beach. I must have picked her up at least three or four times in just a few days. After a while, I would just walk down towards the water when I saw her going in so I could get to her before she went under. I felt sorry for her, but she sure was a bitch when she woke up each time.

Tedium And The Cruel Bottom Line

ANDY B. ('65-'70) - It's natural that we overlook in our recollection that the vast majority of our time was spent sitting. Sitting for up to seven or eight hours on a hard, oak bench that was whitewashed with semi-gloss to keep the splinters down to a minimum, all added up to boredom. No matter how we tried to fend it off by taking short walks, chatting with the patrons, or exchanging war stories with bench partners, the tedium of the job eventually had its day and took us over. Boredom became such a staple of the job that, at times, I could almost become desperate, especially when the battery-operated AM radio reminded me that it was 3:00 p.m. (close to quitting time for a normal job) and that for me, the day was barely half over. Too many days were like that.

The physical trappings of the job didn't help. When I was breaking in during the mid-'60s, we still wore heavy, cloth swimsuits—the extra-slow drying kind. One of the reasons many of us avoided morning workouts was due to our dreaded fear of getting them wet, because then, of course, we had to return to the hardwood bench where our suit would eventually dry, with the exception of that part of the suit that we were sitting on. Within an hour, the intolerable itching would begin. I, for one, tried everything to deal with it: taking short walks, ineffectually shifting from cheek to cheek, even applying talcum powder with my coat pulled over my lap—what a sight that must have been. Some of us even tried sitting on cushions or rolled up towels. No matter: nothing really worked. As lunch time approached, our dignity and our resolve simultaneously fell by the wayside as we resorted to the only sure-fire solution: scratching—scratching long and deeply—until the pain overcame the itch, and we found relief at last. Enough of this memory.

Then there was the wind. A typical summer day would start out with a mild and caressing southerly breeze. By about 12:15, usually right on the money, that breeze would begin to stiffen, and by 2:00 it was blowing steady at about fifteen to twenty miles per hour, some-times harder. Sometimes it blew so hard that the coarse sand, so beau-tifully white and gleaming on a calm day, was transformed into billions of tiny stinging missiles. Then all but the hardiest of the patrons would flee to their bungalows, with a few tough survivors crouching behind canvas windbreaks. We sought refuge on the chair, inches above the reach of this razor sharp dust storm, with our legs being stung to red-ness whenever circumstances forced us to leave the bench.

The afternoon wind wasn't a dry wind either. It usually carried with it a briny dampness that penetrated and touched everything. Sunglasses were constantly fogged and wet, our boyishly long hair was blown into a mass of salty wet tangles, faces were sandblasted to a sore redness, and our heavy wool coats became wet, sandy heaps and seem-ingly stayed that way through Labor Day. We simply could not get them dry after the first week of the season.

Throw a boring bench partner into this mix of circumstances, and the situation could become dire. I spent too many hours dealing with Einsteins whose conversational range was limited to fabricating stories of drunkenness and sexual conquests and whose main source of amuse-ment came from sending hapless, young, teenage girls from stand to stand to search for inane, phantom objects like "the key to the oar-locks" or "twenty-five feet of shoreline."

I was never a moralist, but these brainless, practical jokes always seemed to have an edge of macho sadism that left me squirming with embarrassment for my association with these clowns. And feeling sorry for the victims. Having a bright and interesting bench partner was not merely a blessing—it was a necessity—an insurance policy against the stir craziness that intensified as the season wore on.

Bluefish Frenzy

MICKEY H. - Everyone that ever spent any time on the Jersey Shore knew what a bluefish was and had some type of bluefish story.

If you grew up at the beach, you ate bluefish. They were one of the staple foods. Pound for pound, bluefish are one of the meanest, most ferocious fish in the ocean. They often travel in large schools, like a pack of overgrown piranhas.

When they went into a feeding frenzy, they would just churn up the water. More than once, I remember hauling the tourists out of the water as I saw a school of bluefish churning up the sea as they moved up the beach. Although I never heard of it happening, I figured they could easily take off a finger or a little kid's foot by mistake when they were feeding.

The churning white splashes of the feeding bluefish also created fishermen-feeding frenzies. Tourist fishermen would run into the middle of the swimming area, casting out these huge, three-barbed hooks on the end of a lure and reeling them in through the middle of the swimmers. They always acted like we were crazy when we ran up to them to tell them that they could not fish among the swimmers. They seemed to have no comprehension of the fact that they had as much chance of hooking a swimmer as they did of hooking a bluefish.

Reckless Fishermen

GORDON H. - When I was old enough to hold a surf-fishing pole, my father gave me a few lessons on how to cast and feed the line onto the reel so it wouldn't backlash when casting. Part of the lesson was to watch behind you when you were ready to cast to make sure you were not swinging a fishing hook right into the path of an unwitting beachcomber. I have been amazed, over the years, how often I have seen "green" fishermen throw back their pole and three feet of line without ever looking behind them. I'm sure there must be a few people that have been snagged and possibly seriously injured by such carelessness.

Shooting Boredom

JON S. ('66-'74) - To keep from getting bored on the stand, we'd take water pistols and fire them from behind our backs and hit the people sunbathing nearby. They'd feel little drops, like it was raining, and look up at the blue sky and wonder where the drops came from.

Kenny C. could shoot smooth, shell shards or bottle caps. He could flip them with amazing speed and accuracy. The people would feel this tiny spray of sand and not know what had happened.

July 18, 1967 - Captain's Notice #1

Guards and Police: It has been noted that certain people are using the phone for long periods of time and quite often. Personal calls should be no longer than 2 minutes.

Free Speech

GORDON H. - To keep the work amusing on a slow day, you would play a prank on your bench partner (particularly a rookie). When he left the stand, you would call a buddy on another beach and tell him to ring you back in one or two minutes. Then, he was to disguise his voice and call your partner all kinds of nasty names.

Before he called back, you'd unscrew the cover to the bottom part of the phone and remove the module that converted speech to electric impulse. Then you'd screw the cover back on. When the phone rang, you'd hand it to your bench partner and tell him it was for him. He'd get all this foul language and not be able to respond so the people at the other end could hear him.

Benchless Partners

RUSSELL F. - In the old days, we didn't work out like they do now. We would show up in the morning and relax on the stand. If one of the guys had a hangover, one would be on the bench and the other would lie down on a blanket. Goddard never came up on the beach. He had an old Lincoln Zephyr. He would drive to the corner and never get out of his car. He just looked from the end of each street. I don't think he ever went swimming.

Two-piece Leak

JON S. - A woman went out to get her son. He was on a mat, and he was in a run. She got stuck in the run too, and I ran out for her with the can. By this time, her kid had gotten to the sandbar and come in all right. When I got to her, she started, "I don't need any help. I'm fine." Bitch, bitch, bitch—the whole way in on the can. A crowd had gathered on the beach. When we got to waist deep water, she was sputtering. I saw these kids who were giggling and noticed she was wearing a two-piece bathing suit. From leaning on the can, the top part of her bathing suit had pulled up and exposed her breasts. With all the crap this lady gave me, I wasn't going to say squat. She had to be wondering what all these people were laughing at.

Dashing From The Dance Of Death

DAVE M. (late '60s, '74) - Probably the scariest rescue I ever had was a young girl. It was in Seaside Park, right near the amusement pier. A girl had gotten separated from her raft, and she began to go under. I almost lost her. I got to her just as she went under. When we got her to the beach, she was unconscious. Just as we were about to give her mouth-to-mouth, she sputtered and coughed and immediately stood up and ran off, embarrassed.

Red Or White

JOHN V. ('66-'70) - We used to go to Jon's and sit around drinking beer and playing games. Then we got into Ripple (a cheap, carbonated wine sold in six-packs). Do you remember when we got into red Ripple and white Ripple? Then we started to drink Bali High—that was a step up for us.

Fixing Snyder's Ass

ANDY B, - Another day, Duke came to work with a ridiculous looking bathing cap with sherbet-colored rubber flowers growing out of it. When I asked him about it, he said, "Ah'm gonna fix Snahder's ass."

Snyder was a new guard who was universally disliked.

Around mid-morning Duke put on the cap, entered the water, and swam three blocks to Snyder's beach, the whole way keeping his back to the shore. Upon reaching the beach, he turned around, far enough out so that his face with the broad rounded nose covered with white zinc oxide was unrecognizable. Then he started splashing in the manner of a drowning person. By now, everyone on the beach seemed to be in on the game except Snyder. His bench partner told him that, as the rookie, he had to make the rescue. After Snyder grudgingly left the stand, Duke immediately turned his back to the shore—something that a drowning person never does—and waited. When he heard the splashing of the approaching rescuer, he whirled around and sneered: "Surprahze, Snahder, what took ya so long?"

One can only imagine the comedy of that face, with its bulbous white nose and five o'clock shadow, enshrouded in that garish bathing cap dripping with gaudy rubber flowers. Snyder's reaction was to let out a curse, and he started to swim in by himself. This enraged Duke, who informed him that this was a drill they were involved in, and that if Snyder knew what was good for him, he would complete the mock rescue as directed. And so the farce was played out: a surly Snyder stroking toward the shore where a crowd of tourists had gathered to watch the spectacle—this guard, pulling a torpedo buoy, over which was draped this comical-looking man in a bathing cap, grinning like a madman.

Unpaid Overtime

KENNY J. ('67-'69) - One rainy day, we were supposed to close the beach. A whole family showed up from Ohio, and they had never seen the ocean before. They had just jumped out of the car in the rain and headed for the water. I went down and told them they couldn't go in. They pleaded with me to let them go—this would be their only chance. So I let them go in anyway and watched them for about half an hour. The water wasn't that rough.

Death From Above

TOM A. - One day when it was raining, I was parked at the end of the street. I want to say I was with Sam Hammer. I had a '64 Mustang convertible. It was a big storm. Lightning hits the telephone pole right where we're parked and throws a piece of wood—it had to be two or three feet long and maybe two or three inches wide and thick—right on top of the hood of the car. A few more feet and it would have come through the roof. You talk about getting the shit scared out of you. Holy Christ! I tell you, it was so goddamn loud. And I said to myself, 'We're supposed to be safe—that's why we're sitting here in our cars?' Because they used to say, "take off your belt" (because of the big metal ring on the rescue belts), and make such a big deal about it, because of the guard that had been hit by lightning and killed in Manasquan.

The Rescue In The Middle Of The Night

DICK H. ('50-2000; Captain '66-'80) - It was after the bars closed—after 2:30 in the morning. A couple got drunk and went in swimming in the middle of the night. They couldn't get back in. She was way, way out there. Her boyfriend, who played the piano in the Lavallette Hotel, came and got us. We went out for the girl. In fact, it was a good thing I got there because I knew where the boat and oars were. Frank B. and I rowed out in the boat to get her. We were way out. We had trouble finding her. We kept calling and calling. They had the lights from the fire trucks out shining on the water. She was a fairly decent swimmer, so she was all right, but she was tired when we got her. Her boyfriend was on the beach.

Fanny Dunkers

JON S. - We used to have the posts on the shore with ropes to the posts out in the water. And the big, old, heavy women hung on the ropes, and they'd get washed by a wave and get under the rope and get caught and be gagging. Invariably, they'd get on the side with the waves washing into the rope. They could find more ways to get fouled up. You'd run down to help them, and they were like jelly on one side— you couldn't find a bone anywhere. It was like a big blob. Invariably they were wearing a black bathing suit with flowers.

Beer Vultures

JIMMY A. - It was always like that at the parties. Some of the veteran guards always got at least one new person drunk each night— whoever—a rookie—playing something like "Whales Tales." They would get them drunk. Getting them drunk wasn't a planned thing, you just knew it would happen to someone. They were like vultures waiting for the carcass. You never realized it was your night until it was too late. I remember Paul dropping me off after a party at Jake's. I got to the middle of Route 35 and didn't know which way to go. I couldn't tell the way home even though it was less than two hundred feet away.

A Master Of Deceit

TOM A. - I spent a lot of time with Paul T. He was great for wearing mirror sunglasses and falling asleep while sitting on top of the stand with his arms folded looking as though he was actually watching the water. He was also great for just letting everybody go exactly wherever they wanted to go. And I'd keep saying, "Paul, they're all over the place." And he'd say, "Don't worry about it—I can swim."

Lofty Discussion

TOM A. - *There* was another guy who was crazy. Andy B. was never sober. It was amazing to me that he could function the way he did when you consider what he did to himself. But you always felt safe with Andy—he could make the boat do anything—and Andy could swim. Andy had no qualms about going to sleep on the stand—they were that good that they could go to sleep. Our eyes were always going, but those guys knew they could get away with it.

Andy had a great sense of humor. I always enjoyed sitting with him. Always a great conversation working with him. Conversation ranged from the girl sitting in front of the stand to how to save the world.

False Accusation

GORDON H. - I met a really nice girl named Lani on the beach. She was cute—I liked her so much that I mustered the courage to ask her for a date. That night, I took her to a party at Jake's. Somehow, we had arrived in Andy's parents' '59 Chevy. It was early enough in the season that not all the beaches were open. About four other guards and their dates were playing some silly-ass drinking game like "Thumper" or "Prince of Wales" or "Buzz, Ding." The games were all designed to make novices drink a lot more than they wanted to. My date drank a lot fast and began to get sick. So I took her up to the beach for fresh air. Meanwhile, Andy got plastered. I ended up loading Andy into his car, nearly passed out, dropping off my date, and then watching Andy revive himself just long enough to barf out the passenger side window and down the side of the car as I drove him to his home. I left him and his parents' car at his house and ran home. The next morning on the beach, he was pissed at me. "The least you could have done was clean up the car after your date threw up all over the side," he said. "My parents took the car to church before they knew it was a mess, and I got in a heap of trouble." He couldn't remember a thing except my date getting sick hours before we left the party.

The Strongest Swimmer I Ever Met

JOHN M. ('46-'53; Captain '52-'53) - The strongest swimmer I ever saw was Al Raub. He had very big shoulders and a thin waist, and he could swim like you wouldn't believe.

I remember one time on a rescue, the line got tangled. Back then, we had a large reel mounted on a spindle on a tripod. It probably weighed nearly sixty pounds. Normally, it would feed out the line, but Raub swam out at an angle, and the rope got twisted around the spindle. Raub ended up pulling the whole reel out into the water.

We used to have fish pounds way offshore. Raub would swim out to them almost every day. I used to row out with him.

Caves I And II

CHARLIE B. ('65, '67-'71) - We rented a basement apartment for $600.00 per month, but they had a rear house that wasn't rented out. We used it for the overflow (from the parties). That was where we had the garbage can parties. We put everything in the cans. Then we got smart and started to use trashcan liners. That cut down on the alcohol reacting with the galvanized cans. A barber once asked where I got the scars on my scalp. I told him it was from the garbage can parties.

Rusty and I had a bet going on who could get laid the most times in one night. Rusty got laid four times, but the best I could do was two Lebanese sisters.

The Lebanese Sisters

CHARLIE B. - I invited these two sisters. Somebody had some kind of Hawaiian lei or necklace made out of this stuff that got on one of the beds. It got crumbled up and looked like confetti. I had gotten laid by these two Lebanese sisters during the night. Neither one knew about the other.

How'd I do it? How do I know—I was drunk and stupid. They must have been drunker and stupider.

Back then, I never used condoms; I'd just pull out at the critical moment. In the morning when I got up, though, that confetti had gotten on the bed and stuck to all the sticky parts. I had a hell of a job getting it all off my privates.

Quick Exits

PATRICIA D. - One of the reasons I was in and out of the lifeguard shack in the morning was that I didn't want to hear about what they did the night before, if they could remember it. I signed in and got out in a hurry.

Conducting Tourists

GORDON H. - As guards, we were always happy to see lightning since it meant we could take off our belts with their brass buckles, tell people to get out of the water, and advise them to leave the beach until the lightning had passed. Though usually brief, it gave us a rest from vigilance.

Lightning over the ocean can be spectacular. The uninterrupted view of dark clouds discharging and the flashes hitting the ocean less than a mile offshore is awe-inspiring. But at the first sign of rain, many people huddled under their metal umbrellas, not realizing that they were sitting under a virtual lightning rod in the midst of a very flat plain.

Near-Drowning In An Inch Of Water

JIM C. ('67-present; Captain '81-present) - When I was twelve years old or so, I remember on White Avenue a little boy with a mask on who was snorkeling and looking for shells and things. And I think the mask filled up with water, and he was still floating. Finally, somebody said, "Check that kid." The guard—it was The Whale—ran down and pulled him out of the water. That was probably the first CPR that was given here. He ripped the mask off and cleaned out all the mucus and sand. He got the kid breathing and revived him.

Closing The Beach

SAM H. ('62-'68) - Jimmy A. and I were working down the south end of town, maybe Beach #5. It was a crummy day, and we had the boat on its side. We were drinking and drinking, and it got to be 6:00 p.m., and we didn't even go in. We just stayed there—we were having a hell of a time. I think we finally just pulled the oar out from underneath the boat and left everything there.

Low Overhead

PAUL T. ('66-'73) - One day, Sam and I got so drunk under the lifeguard boat, we stayed on the beach until 8:00 at night. We left everything there, the phone and gear. We were comfortable, so why leave?

July 20, 1967 - Captain's Notice #2

Philadelphia Ave. or any Ave. are not drag strips or racetracks. Any more pealing out and the local police will be at the finish line giving out tickets. One of the local sport fans phoned in the results.

Captain's Notice Author

ANDY B. - Some of us fought the tedium by drinking away the long afternoons, not something that I mention with any degree of pride. Compared to today's guards, we were older. Also, during the '60s, people were rebellious against anything that smacked even remotely of authority. Our captain, Dick Hoffman, possessed the perfect disposition for this zeitgeist. He had spent many years sitting on the bench as "one of the guys" before finally making it to lieutenant in 1965 at age thirty-six. He was very skilled at getting us to do things his way without being abrasive and at the same time imparting his own brand of humor.

Dick was well known for posting frequent "bulletins" over the course of the summer, most of them chastising us for our various indiscretions. These included (but were not limited to): going fishing in the Hankins skiffs during off hours; taking the skiffs out wave riding at night after getting ourselves falling-down drunk ("I was too drunk to walk officer, I had no choice but to row home."); running the skiffs onto jetties and putting costly holes in them; excessively talking to the "split-tails" (otherwise known as "snappers"); taking excessively long head breaks or lunches; leaving the stand for no good reason; leaving the beach for no good reason (usually to have a "taste" of beer at a beachfront house); or, the occasional mortal sin of not showing up for work at all. Dick addressed all of these ventures from the straight and narrow with language that was salty, humorous, and scathingly sarcastic. If somebody screwed up, and this happened nearly every day, we all knew about it instantly and looked for the bulletin, which we knew would be waiting for us at day's end. A typical Hoffman original would read something like this: *"It has been noticed recently that some of you RINKY STINKS, masquerading as gods, have been spending way too much time talking it up with the SPLIT-TAILS. If this continues, some of you RINKY STINKS are going to have all the time in the world to spend with your precious SNAPPERS, and I guarantee that you'll get tired of it real quick...etc., etc."*

A Father's Gallantry

GORDON H. - One day we had a ferocious shorebreak. The waves built and then smashed hard onto the steep angle of the shore, quickly draining back into the ocean, sometimes with such force that it would pull people over.

A young father had gotten into the water with his three-year old, but when he started to come out, he mistimed when to sprint out. The draining water slowed him down enough that he could not beat the building and oncoming wave behind him. As the looming wave hit him with full force in the back, he gallantly raised his son above the torrent as he was driven across the shells and stones of the lower beach on his chest. He spun around with his precious package held above the dangers, like a football held across the goal, while his son giggled with delight at the fantastic ride. As the dad cleared the water, he set his son down on his feet and stood up himself. His chest streamed a series of bloody rivulets as his son gleefully cheered, "That was fun. Do it again, Daddy!"

July 23, 1967 - Captain's Notice #3
Certain guards are still using the phone
quite often and for long periods of time.
Again, personal calls should be no longer
than 2 minutes.

Guards - It has been the practice for years that
guards eat on the stands Sat., Sun., and holidays
unless notified. Beach 6 please take note!
Thank you.

Guards - Also it has been reported by you
know who—yesterday on two beaches. #4 was
mentioned that a snapper was inside the roped
off area around the stand. At this one beach it
was reported that she was there 10 minutes.
2 minutes is the length of time for a snapper.

Rescue Digest

GORDON H. - When the surf and current were particularly rough on a weekend, the guards sometimes were not allowed to leave the beach for lunch. One day my partner, Andy, and I had not completed arrangements for lunch to be delivered until early afternoon. We were both famished. Finally, about 1:30 p.m., my father brought us some Mike's Subs (now Jersey Mike's) submarine sandwiches. Andy began to eat first. Almost before he was finished, I began to eat. Then it happened! Two kids got caught in an undertow and began yelling. Andy and I looked at each other for an instant trying to figure out who should go first. Andy said, "I'll go."

He got to the kids quickly and after swimming to the side of the undertow, got them safely ashore. When he got back to the bench he still had lettuce streaming from his mouth and cheeks.

What Comes Around

SAM H. - Ritter worked as John T.'s bench partner. He's an FBI guy now. One year, Ritter tried to organize a half-assed strike for more money for the guards. When the FBI did a background check on him, that came up. He was a big conservative: he gave me Barry Goldwater's *The Conscience of a Conservative.*

The Man With The Movie Camera

GORDON H. - A father on vacation had his eye glued to the eyepiece of his 8-mm movie camera. He must have thought he was Cecil B. DeMille. He was so engrossed in keeping his son in focus that he did not notice that the boy was being carried out in a run and beginning to show the first signs of distress. My partner clipped on the can and began rushing toward the surf. Out of the corner of his eye, the father saw the guard and decided to get action footage of a rescue. He must have thought the home movie would be elevated to documentary status.

My partner dove in and came up just feet from the man's son. It looked like the father was thrilled by this exciting moment in his vacation until, through the viewfinder, he saw the guard shove the torpedo buoy to his boy. At that moment, his head recoiled as if the camera had become a discharging shotgun. Mortified, he walked down into the surf as his rescued son was brought ashore, none the worse for wear, if not a little shaken by how quickly the current had taken him beyond his capacities and how his father had been oblivious to his situation.

Stingrays

MICKEY H. - I did not see another stingray until I was guarding in Lavallette nearly twenty years after my father had speared one. I was working one of the southern beaches on one of those beautiful days when the water was warm, calm, and clear. It had a real tropical feeling. All of a sudden, I noticed some large black patches slowly moving along the bottom. I hauled the tourists out of the water and went out in the boat to check it out. Sure enough, it was a small school of the large rays. Since they were not sharks, I let the tourists back in. Some of the rays were in chest-deep water in the same area that the tourists were walking in. I spent the rest of the day keeping the tourists and the stingrays apart. If someone stepped on one of those big rays, and it whipped its tail up, they would be getting a jagged, six-inch long barb in the crotch. I did not even want to think about dealing with that situation. I know most of the tourists had no idea of why I was moving them around so much on a calm day or what they were sharing the swimming area with. The next day, I came to work with my father's spear and a facemask, but the rays were able to sense something was different, and they never let me get close enough to spear them.

Ship To Shore

PAUL T. - John M. and I were on the beach and watched this scallop boat drifting in all day. His engines were out, and he kept drifting in and drifting in. He dumped his load of scallops somewhere. The waves were pretty big. Every time a big wave hit the boat, it would spray out and the people on the beach would go, *"Oooooh!"* Finally, we rowed out to get the one guy on the boat off. The guy was all drunked up. We finally got him to jump off, and he went straight to the bottom. I think John went in and got him. We had a devil of a time getting him into the boat. It was tough getting in close enough because of the waves. We were worried we'd break up against the boat.

A Drowning At The Surf Club

GORDON H. - I'd never worked on a beach that had lost a person to drowning until I guarded at the Surf Club. It was a small nightclub less than a half mile from Lavallette with only a few hundred feet of riparian rights. It had a reputation as a den of iniquity, and my experiences there confirmed that the label was earned. On weekends, the club was jammed until the wee hours of the morning. During the day, people would link up with people they had met the night before and often continue drinking.

There were three guards on duty at any time the beach was open. When I began working there, we had gotten disparaging comments from the neighboring township beaches which flanked the club. They seemed to have a low opinion of our abilities until we assisted each other on a day when the surf was very rough. That day, we established that we had the chops to guard. We celebrated with them at the end of the day with drinks at the bar. It was then that I learned that a drowning had taken place at the Surf Club the year before, and this had been what had given them the impression that we were substandard. It would not be for another year before I actually met the guard that was on duty and learned the whole story.

He told me that this man had been drinking in the bar all Sunday long with a large group of friends. Late in the afternoon, he decided to go in for a dip. He charged into the water, turned around, walked up on the beach, and keeled over. Dead. Right in front of the lifeguards.

I was told that the guards later learned that the man was so inebriated that when he dove in, involuntary muscles did not stop the water from going into his lungs, and that was enough to drown the man.

Double-ball Hangouts

GORDON H. - People taking vacation photos would often use the lifeguard bench as a backdrop to their pictures. The typical picture would be of one or two children, smiling at the camera with their pail and shovel or rafts. Almost invariably, the lifeguards' image would be cut off—sometimes at the feet or the chest.

The first time I recall being part of the background, my veteran partner spread his legs so that one testicle flowed out one side of the lining of his bathing suit, and the other protruded on the opposite side. Grinning broadly at the camera—which he knew would not include his face—he delighted at the perverse prospect of what the photographer would see behind the heads of his subjects when his film came back from processing weeks later.

The Lifeguard Ball

JOHN M. - Back in the early 1950s, all summer long we used to sell tickets to the Lifeguard Ball. The tickets were only $2.00 or $3.00 and that entitled you to get through the door at the Red Rail Restaurant and pay for your drinks and meal. We didn't put the money in the bank; we used to give shares based on the number of nights you went out to sell tickets. One year, we raised over $3,000.00 worth of tickets. The shares might have been worth about $20.00 a piece. Guys that worked all sixteen nights could make almost as much money as they did all summer long.

But then they shut it down. The cops and the fireman would say, "The lifeguards are taking all the money. We go around trying to collect money, and they say they already gave to the lifeguards." So they made us stop and that ended the Lifeguard Ball.

July 24, 1967 - Captain's Notice #4

Guards - When you take a pith break, phone out right away—you don't need 10 minutes before. If you do, get your plumbing checked.

Sunday, four leakers left the beach and were in the office, and not one raised their hand to leave the room.

Handwriting On The Wall

Lifeguard Headquarters Bathroom Etiquette by Bob

Rule #1   When paper roll is empty, put a new roll on the roller.

Rule #2   If there's not another roll sitting right in front of your face waiting to be put on, then reach up on the shelf and get another one down.

Rule #3   If you can't reach or see toilet paper up on the shelf, "Put the lid down" (very important) and step up so you can reach or see.

Rule #4   If after stepping up on the toilet, you still can't reach or see, maybe you should find a ladder.

Rule #5   When you can finally see on the shelf, and there is no paper there, "Don't keep it a secret." We don't want to put the next person through the same thing you just went through, especially if he/she doesn't realize there's no paper until it's too late!

Fishing Expedition

JOHN M. - One time, The Whale, Art M., and Eddie V. thought they would be real smart and put an outboard on the back of the surf-boat and packed it with fishing poles and went fishing. But they didn't bother to put oars in the boat, which was real bad because there was a strong west wind. At some point after they got out a ways, they tried to start the motor. The Whale pulled the starter cord so hard it came off. They were stranded.

That evening after dinner, I went up to the boardwalk and noticed the boat with the three of them way out there. I watched them for a while and then realized they were dead in the water. I grabbed four oars and rowed out to them. Of course, I didn't give them the oars until I had totally humiliated them. They were helpless.

Hammerhead Shark

MICKEY H. - In 1974, I was guarding in Ocean Beach when they had a shark scare. I was the senior-most guard on the beach and had the younger guys really pumped about going out in the boat. Every time we had a possible shark scare, there was a rush to get to the boat to see who would get to go out after it. This time, Tom M. and I got to the boat first. We rowed out about a quarter mile to where we saw another guard boat from a nearby beach. After looking around for just a few minutes, a seven-food hammerhead shark popped up right next to our boat.

The other boat high-tailed it to the beach, but we gave chase. Hell, I was in a Hankins boat and felt invincible. I figured there was not much a seven-foot shark could do to an eight hundred-pound boat. It definitely would have been a different situation if I ever fell over the side. I got in the front of the boat with an oar balanced in my hand like Captain Ahab. I kept telling Tom to row harder so we could get close enough so I could hit the shark. I don't know why I wanted to bother the shark; it just seemed like the thing to do at the time. After chasing it for about fifteen minutes, Tom was exhausted and complaining because there was a leak in the boat, and we were rapidly filling up with water. So, I finally hurled the oar like a harpoon and hit the shark in the back. He just quietly disappeared. We then had to haul ass to the nearest beach to get the water out of the boat since we could not have gotten back to our beach with all the water that was sloshing around our ankles.

Island Party

GORDON H. - On the western side of Lavallette is Barnegat Bay. Not far from its shores are two islands. One, West Point Island, has been developed and is now considered Lavallette's idea of the "ritzy" side of town. The other, Hank's Island (a.k.a. Mosquito Island), is on the north end of town and is about two hundred feet wide and a little more than one hundred feet across the channel from the Yacht Club. With the exception of a small clearing in the center, it is overgrown with andropogon and tall weeds.

By the third year we had been guarding, Andy and I were among the only senior lifeguards who were not engaged or of drinking age, so we began using Hank's Island for our parties, which tended to be small—perhaps ten to fifteen people to keep the logistics simple and the risk of getting raided by the police small.

We held two parties there that year. My cousin, who is only a year older and very attractive, had stopped by earlier that evening with a girlfriend looking for some excitement, and I had invited them to the party we were planning. We had two boats ferry about fifteen people to the island, which was less than half a mile from the public dock where we had gathered.

For lack of other entertainment, once everyone had drunk several beers, we played spin the bottle. When the idea first came up, I thought we were taking a giant step back toward high school. But it got interesting. No one wanted to look like they were inexperienced, and the other participants gave boos or applause based upon what they considered the quality of the kisses exchanged. Unlike the high school version, we were all beyond the "kiss and tell" stage and deep meaningful embraces with exploratory kisses replaced the younger, more innocent pecks. When my cousin and I kissed, it had an incestuous excitement.

Afterward, Andy had linked up with Renee who sort of became his "date" for the evening. A perky and beautiful woman-child, with long dark hair, she was about eighteen or ninteen and had gotten drunk and could not stop laughing. Everything seemed funny to her. Of course, Andy got pretty drunk too, but he was at least at the functional level. When they motored back to the dock in a Boston Whaler to take everyone home, Andy helped lift the ladies up to the dock which was chest high to the people in the boat. While holding onto the dock with one hand, he grabbed Renee around the waist to lift her up. This set her off laughing uncontrollably—perhaps in her state she thought he was tickling her. The next moment, Andy was trying to hold onto the dock, and the Whaler began to drift away. I have this mental snapshot of Andy's distress and Renee's laughter reaching a pitch when she had a glimmer of what was inevitable. They both tumbled into the chest deep water, with Renee continuing to laugh upon resurfacing. She was about the happiest and most enjoyable drunk I ever saw.

On The Value Of Surfboats On Dry Land

MICKEY H. - Boats could also be useful at night when they were turned upside down beyond the high-water mark. One night, Tommy and Gary were drinking heavily and realized late at night that if they went to sleep, they would never be able to get up in time for work because they were close to passing out. To solve the dilemma, they drove to the guard shack and crawled under the lifeguard boat in front of the shack and passed out. When everyone arrived in the morning, they could see their car, but could not find them. When they finally opened the beach and flipped over the boat they found them asleep under the boat, in uniform, ready to go to work.

<u>July 26, 1967 - Captain's Notice #5</u>
It has been reported, and I have watched a few times myself, that some beaches are pulling out early. Please keep your cans and box on the beach until you get called in. Everything else can be pulled in.

Oh, yes, pictures are in. Bring in the cash and you can get your photos in the office.

Porpoises

GORDON H. - Almost every summer a school of porpoises would swim by the beach and cause a lot of excitement. There were always a few idiots who thought they were sharks despite their rhythmic breathing arcs.

One day, when the waves were about three feet tall on the incoming tide, two or three porpoises rode the waves toward the beach. Everyone on the beach and boardwalk was mesmerized by these beautiful mammals and their playfulness as they skimmed along the waves. When they got close to the shore and turned out of the waves to continue their journey, the beach erupted in spontaneous applause.

Mistaken Identity

TOM A. - Seaside Heights had called and said that they had spotted a shark moving in our direction. We were told to keep an eye out for it. We gave the signal to the people on the beach to stay in close. We were looking through glasses to see if we could see anything. We were watching and watching. We just happened to see this thing sticking up through a wave as it broke. It was one of those bat kites that just happened to be floating out there. The wind was blowing out of the west and held up one of the wings. It looked like a fin. One of our guys swam out to it—I don't know if it was Paul or Andy—and started "wrestling" with it. There were people on the beach going, "Oh, my God, look at him out there, wrestling with the shark!"

Drowning Headfirst

GORDON H. - Now, much of the bottom of much of Barnegat Bay is oozing mud. When we dug for cherrystone clams with our feet, in some spots, we would sink in the mud almost to our knees. I remember hearing the rumor of a macabre drowning that took place off one of the lagoons on the bay in Ortley, the next town over. It was at night, and apparently there was drinking. Anyway, at this party someone supposedly dove in headfirst. Their head stuck in the mud, and because their hands had nothing solid to push against, they could not get free and drowned. For some reason, the idea of drowning inverted like that seems even more horrible.

Hunch Punch

BOBBI A. ('65-'69) - The first Viking parties started at Sammy's when they made Hunch Punch. They would throw a bunch of fruit juices in a garbage can and add booze. Then once in a while we would have a health night and stay at home.

Party Houses

MICKEY H. - It seemed that every summer there was at least one party house. Usually it was rented by at least four or more guards. There would usually be a full-on hunch punch party there every few weeks. Hunch punch parties got their name from the fact that you often only had a hunch about what was in the punch that you were drinking. The hosts would buy a brand new plastic trashcan, ice, and a few gallons of punch. Everyone that came to the party would bring a bottle of hard liquor and pour it into the trashcan along with the punch and ice and then stir it around. Mixtures were wild and of varying strengths and tastes. Sometimes you could drink several cups with only a minor impact, while other times a single cup would set you off. I can remember seeing some really drunk people at those parties. Once I tried to talk a girlfriend into jumping from the roof and attempting to land in the hunch punch can, but she was not drunk enough to go along with it.

Usually these parties were fairly easy to cleanup afterwords: just pick up the plastic cups and empty bottles and wash out the trashcan.

<u>July 29, 1967 - Captain's Notice #6</u>

Guards - It has been noted that some pith breaks are from "25 to 35" minutes long. I'm sure if you don't have to crap, it's poor policy to sit and force it. That is how you get piles, not from the hard stools. Pith breaks should be 10 or 15 minutes. Remember there are gas stations, and friends' homes are close by.

AGAIN - The pictures are in. Get up the green stuff and you can get yours.

De-evolving Viking Parties

JOHN V. - The Viking parties started out neat. You'd eat a nice dinner and *then* start throwing food. At the end, it got to the point where you'd walk in, and in the first five minutes, they just started throwing food all over the place. Hardly anyone got to eat.

The Sandbar Washed Out

JACK C. - My worst rescue was on Beach #3. That's the one between Guyer Avenue and President Avenue, which is notoriously calm. We had two people in the water. It was flowing south to north. Then there was a set of waves that washed out the entire sandbar, and with the way the water started ripping, everybody started moving north. The sand washed out. The sandbar wasn't there anymore—that's how much power the waves had. And then the people we were trying to keep from heading south to north were now heading north to south. All of a sudden, they were heading in the opposite direction! It was scary, and the people were terrified.

We ended up taking out two lines and surfboards. We had everything out.

Lifeguard Tournament, 1980. In this tournament boating event, lifeguards scramble in rough surf to avoid getting struck by a surfboat in the wash.

August

Seasoning

It is as if the summer turns a corner when August arrives. The air often takes on a dry feel to it. The surf becomes more temperamental. As the month progresses, the late summer flowers blossom, spilling a waft of melancholy.

On the beach, bench partners have established rituals to setting up the guarding apparatus. A sense seems to develop that all living must be squeezed into the diminishing days of summer. Parties, overindulgence, part time jobs, and too many late nights all begin to take their toll. Slights earlier overlooked now become antagonisms.

Rainy days are cherished as an opportunity to rest the eyes from vigilance. A day spent under a partially overturned boat braced with oars can provide time for treasured sleep, to read, to write letters, to spend time with girlfriends, or to drink. Some of the guards leave in late August for college and late-season rookies or old time lifeguards take a shot at a few days back on the bench.

The beach scene becomes more reflective in August. Events quick-

ly become memories—some to be carelessly tossed aside in a day or two, others taking on a luster with time. Deep in the back of many people's minds is the thought, "These will, one day, be the good ol' days."

♠ ♠ ♠

Swimming The Line

JACK C. ('77-present) - Once the line started to get a bow, you were gassing. That's why now we recommend using the fins—even when the line gets a bow, your legs can bring you home. I remember when they said you couldn't use fins.

Now we do a lot of training, so the guys can get the fins on fast when they're rushing on a rescue.

Surfboat Wipeout

JON S. ('66-'74) - Tom and I did things that I've never seen anybody else do in the boats. We'd do late takeoffs for fun—straight vertical drops. When the beaches were closed, we'd be out there.

Kenny and I were out one morning when the beach was closed. We had to wait to get out...wait to get out...wait to get out...wait...wait...and went for it and just about made it. A set came in, and we saw we weren't going to make it. And we didn't want to get in a situation where the boat would flip. We popped the oars out and put them under the seat. And from what people said on shore, the wave came up, went up high, came down, and the boat was gone, completely covered. It drove us straight down to the bottom.

Fear Factor

KENNY J. ('67-'69) - I enjoyed the boat but found it a little intense, a little intimidating.

Big Day With Jon And Ken

MICKEY H. ('67-'76) - The biggest day I remember going out in a boat was probably with Jon S. and Ken C. in front of the shack. It was at least eight-foot-plus hurricane surf. Bright and sunny, no wind, with big lines coming through. The whole squad was there watching us. Rowing out on a big day is always exciting because you really cannot see the waves coming at you. Jon and I were rowing and Ken was in the stern as we went out. We could tell they were big by the way Ken was smiling as we paddled out toward them. We caught air going over some of the sets. We also took a lot of water from punching through the soup.

When we finally got out, we had to bail before we could go for a wave. We waited and then took off on a set wave. The drop was awesome. Jon and I had to jump back really quickly to keep from pearling. Then, after we made the drop, Jon had to move up to keep the boat trimmed. The whitewater was higher than the sides of the boat and completely filled the boat by the time we reached the beach. We wanted to go out for another ride, but Dick, the captain, said we had to all go to our beach and get to work.

Rowing For Freedom

JACK C. - You talk to the younger guards, they don't understand; but the guys that have been here four or five years love to go out in the boats. There is nothing better than going out for a row. It's so peaceful. Yeah, it's exercise, and you're riding waves, and that's fun too, but to get out there and just row, it's like being free. If you took the boats off the beaches, you'd have some very unhappy people.

Black Day At Island Beach

MICKEY H. - It is hard to watch someone die in front of their wife and children and know that there is nothing you can really do to save them. The year I was at Island Beach State Park, a guy fell over right next to the bench to the north of mine. By the time I could run over, the guards were already giving him cardio-pulmonary resuscitation. Due to its isolation and the large number of tourists that would show up there, the guard squad had its own paramedic and first aid room.

The paramedic soon arrived and took over as we carried the victim up to the first aid room on a backboard while giving him CPR. Although they called for an ambulance immediately, it was a Sunday afternoon, and the roads were jammed up with traffic. It must have taken twenty minutes for them to get there. We were working on him the whole time, but it was obvious he was gone.

The wife was crying and praying and asking when the ambulance was going to arrive. The kids just looked at us like there was something we could do to change things or save him. We were just lifeguards: we could rescue someone in the ocean, but we could not bring back the dead. Later, we found out that he died of a massive cerebral hemorrhage. There was nothing anyone could have done to save him. It was one of the hardest days I have ever had at the beach. I can still remember feeling so helpless while we waited for the ambulance to get there, even though we knew it was too late.

Old "Wild" Bill

ANDY B. ('65-'70) - The lifeguard headquarters was little more than an old sewerage pumping station next to the boardwalk. "Old" Bill Kemble, our phone dispatcher, was a harmonious blend of everyone's grandfather and ancient sea dog. Working in a frenetic environment of youthful hormones and conflict, one-up-manship, ball busting, and braggadocio, Bill was a soothing and tranquil presence. Like the calm eye in the storm, he would sit quietly at a desk with a ledger and a switchboard and duly note the arrival of the guards as they checked in each morning. He would quietly face the ocean through the window across his desktop as the hungover young studs arrived bustling with tales of adventures. Amid the bellyaching and swapping of lies of the previous night's conquests, Bill would sit quietly, sometimes chatting over the day's plans with the captain, sometimes sucking on a huge, ubiquitous cigar until the business end of it took on the consistency of brown paper-maché. At other times, little Bill in his grey khaki shirt and pants uniform would be seen eating brandy-soaked blueberries from a jar with a spoon clutched in his gnarled fist, juice rolling down his stubbled chin. At such moments, Bill was an unassuming and even comical presence.

During head breaks, or other times when you got him alone, Bill would open up, spinning yarns in his unmistakable voice. Its soothing sound recalled hand-rubbed wood and seemed to come from deep in his throat to his thick lips. His voice was so calming that it had the power to slow down the metabolism in even those with a restless swagger.

"Did you ever hear the story about the fella who loved to drink?" He would say, "Oooh, he drank to beat the band. His family was so upset about this that they appointed his brother-in-law to take him aside and talk sense into him. So the brother-in-law gets the idea of taking him to the Ballantine Brewery. So he takes him there at night, and the place, a huge brewery, is all lit up and in full operation. So the brother-in-law says to this fella, 'Just look at the size of this place, you can never hope to drink this place dry.' So the fella answers, 'That's true, but I got'em working overtime, don't I?'"

His story would conclude with Bill giving a series of deep guffaws.

Doubleheader

JON S. - We would call Kemble and tell him that one of us was going out for lunch. A few minutes later, the other partner would call out. When Bill called back, no one answered. He thought the beach was unmanned.

An Ear To The Beach

GORDON H. ('65-'73, '75) - From different clicks on the lines,

Andy and I suspected that Old Bill was eavesdropping on our conversations when he was bored. After all, he was stuck in the guard shack sitting at a switchboard all day, keeping mundane records of the coming and goings of the guards, where ambulances needed to be dispatched to, who needed to go on a head break, and other things of this sort. There were days for him that were just not eventful.

It was sometimes the same sitting on the bench. There wasn't much happening: the water was calm, perhaps the wind had picked up so much that most of the beach had cleared out by four o'clock, and the guards would use the phones to recall adventures and plot new ones. We weren't supposed to use them for personal conversations, but we did, and no one cared as long as we were doing our jobs.

So we decided to smoke Bill out when we thought he was listening in on our conversations. We could sense him, more than hear him, on the line.

We began to tell the most outrageous tale with great embellishment. Then, in the background, our suspicions were confirmed when we heard a muted and uncontrolled but jovial: *"huh, huh."*

It was Bill's unmistakable laugh.

"Bill! What are you doing?!" I demanded gruffly.

"Oh, sorry boys," came his soft voice. "I just pushed down the wrong switch," was his response, followed by a guilty click disconnect.

Drowning Tracks

GORDON H. - Years of watching people on the beach gives an experienced guard a "sixth sense" of things that are out of order. I had heard this from the veteran guards I had met, but only half-believed it until the day I spotted a person drowning on the next beach, perhaps one hundred fifty yards away. I was not even looking in that direction but knew something was wrong. I looked to the guards on that beach. They seemed oblivious: legs crossed and looking up at the clouds. I looked out into the water again. There! Beyond the waves! A person came up from under the surface of the water, flailed for perhaps two seconds, and then went under.

I looked back to the guards on the stand. Still looking up at the clouds! I blew my whistle long and hard. They looked over to me. I pointed to them and then to the place where the person had gone under. Thank God! He came up again, and they saw him—way offshore. There was no way they could get to him in time if he did not come up again.

They dashed off on what was likely to be a futile rescue. Fortunately, another guard was in the water near the victim. When he saw me point to the man, he began swimming. He brought him up and held onto him until the other guards got to him and could assist in bringing him ashore.

In seven years of ocean guarding, I had never seen a person go under without warning in calm water like this man. Later, the guards told me that the man had needle tracks on his arm.

A Late Season Rookie

EDWARDO B. ('69-'70) - I was working on the beach crew with Jimmy. They needed more guards and had a mid-season tryout. Jim and I watched and were laughing at the guys trying out—they nearly drowned. The captain said, "If you can do better, try it." I even did a flip off the bow and got the job.

First partner was Jim C. or Andy. I was alone for fifteen minutes and had my first pull. It wasn't really a pull. She didn't need help, but I made her come in with me.

Disputing A Rescue

JIM C. ('67-present; Captain '81-present) - I was on Trenton Avenue with Joe M. He might have been filling in at lunchtime or something. It was big surf. It was like the Fourth of July. It was maybe the first year I started guarding, and we were just going out and getting people. I went in on one rescue and it seemed like the surf was as high as a flag-pole. This *huge* wave came—and I knew I had to get to the person, so I kinda dug my hands into the bottom of the beach, and—*ba-boom*—it broke on me. I came out and swam to the people and said, "Just relax and hold on." Then I'm waiting for somebody to come out. Nobody came. The next thing I know, I'm trying to get them in, and we're getting smashed. And then I see Joe and Jake (the lieutenant that year) arguing back and forth. Apparently Joe didn't want to go in or didn't think I needed help, and Jake was arguing that he should go in. Finally, they sent someone out, and we got in. They continued to argue, and I think Joe stormed off the beach. I just said, "I'm minding my own business."

Change In The Weather

PAUL T. ('66-'73) - It was a northeastern in 1968. They usually last for three days. The first morning it was nasty—it was blowing at forty miles per hour and raining. They closed the beach altogether. Half the guys went home, and everyone else went to Jake's and started drinking. Around 1:00 or 2:00 in the afternoon, there were breaks in the clouds. By 3:30, the sun came out, and people started flocking to the beach. They had been cooped up in their houses all day. And there was a bad shorebreak and runs. Dick, the captain, started crying. He had tears running down his cheeks. I couldn't tell if it was because the party was over or because he had no sober, experienced lifeguards.

<u>August 4, 1967 - Captain's Notice #7</u>
Guards - On days when it rains, keep the phone in your car. To do this, all you have to do is stretch the wire across the boardwalk.

Some of my sports are still taking advantage of the 1/2 hour lunch. Your lunch period is 1/2 hour, not 35 or 40 minutes. You should be able to punch out on time with the traveling time. If this keeps up, all we will do is dock you for the extra time.

Let's get the $1.00 up for the picture. Mr. Anderson wants the loot; he hasn't had a reading lesson in quite some time. Give up one of your reading lessons or rippling water baths.

Calls With A Twist

JOE S. ('68-'76, '90s, '00s) - There were two lifeguards and myself. We went down to Krone's Bar and Grill and ran a bunch of telephone lines together on a rainy day so we could sit in the bar and drink and still answer the phone for the beach. We wouldn't have gotten caught except some lady backed up over the plug and called the police. That was my last year.

Downtown Lifeguarding

DICK H. ('50-2000; Captain '66-'80) - This is on a rainy day. And all of a sudden I hear on the walkie-talkie from the police that there are wires down coming from the beach. What the hell are they talking about "wires down?" Well, I went to investigate. Three beaches got together—you remember in those days we used to have those telephones and you'd snap the wires together? They'd snapped them together and came all the way down the street into Krone's. They were all sitting there drinking at Krone's.

I didn't discipline any of them. I said, "This is the best one that ever happened as long as I've been lifeguarding—I've never had anything like this happen. But don't let it happen again, or you're goners."

JIM C. - One of the policemen, it might have been Freddie S., said there was a phone line down on Brooklyn or Washington Avenue. Then he came back and said, "Nah, nah, that's okay, it's the lifeguards—it runs from the beach down to Krone's." I can remember Dick and I saying, "Jesus!" They had left one guy on each beach and screwed the lines together. Apparently they had the phone right there on the bar, and they were having cocktails.

A Viking Feast

GORDON H. - One particularly raucous Viking feast and party was at a bayfront home in August. All went well until the first keg was tapped. It was understood that, even though the feast featured such foods as potato salad, corn on the cob, cherrystone clams, and grilled meats, no eating utensils were permitted. That was okay for most of the savvy attendees who came in swimming clothing.

For no particular reason, people started to fling beer at one another, wasting nearly the entire first keg. Then food started to fly. I remember one elegant and classy, but sadly misinformed, young lady in a pristine white blouse getting splattered by a large, greasy steak bone the moment she made her entrance. It got worse. Catsup and mustard bottles began to squirt out their contents. Handfuls of macaroni salad were lumped in people's faces. When it began to escalate, my date and I left for the showers.

The next day, three of the guards reported in late, having had to go to the doctors to get corn and bread extricated from their ears.

Two Stepsisters And Their Little Cousin

HOBIE ('65-'74) - One day C.K., one of my pals, called and asked me if I would be interested in helping him and his little brother out with some nasty young ladies. I said, "Sure," and after work, we went to pick them up. It was a little awkward when we got to their house because it turned out that the oldest two were seventeen-year old stepsisters and their cousin was only fifteen. We were in our early twenties, but my friend's little brother was only fifteen, so we thought it was a pretty good mix. We took them to a party house and got right down to business since they had a 10:00 p.m. curfew.

First, we all had a can of beer since that was all it took to give them a buzz. Next, we split up. C.K. went to one room with his date, and the remaining four of us were in another room with a curtain down the middle to divide it. The curtain did not bother anyone, and we all took off our clothes and got down to business. Before long, the curtain had fallen down, and the four of us were in beds next to each other fucking away. After a little while, we changed partners for a second round. Another guard knocked on the front door, and one of the girls ran up to him with no clothes on and gave him a big kiss on the lips.

She said, "Guess what I taste like?"

"Uh..., marijuana?" he replied.

"No," she replied, "cum!"

He promptly left to wash his mouth and did not return.

Before the evening was over, I remember fingering two of them at the same time. It was a wild night. I guess you might consider it an orgy since there were multiple partners in the same room at the same time. We would have been in a lot of trouble if we had gotten caught by the police with that many underage participants and beer in the same place, but we never thought about those types of things. Those girls may have been young, but they were some of the nastiest I had ever met.

<u>August 7, 1967 - Captain's Notice #8</u>
Guards - Quite a few of you mothers are so anxious to get to your cocktail parties that you are beating the hell out of the stands by running them back and dropping them on their backs. Please keep it cool for a while and lower the stands easy. They are hard to replace. I'm sure the snappers can keep warm a few minutes longer.

There are a few arm benders in this group that still didn't get up the $1.00. Before going out tonight, stick the buck in your pants pocket so you don't forget it tomorrow.
Leaders of the pack: Sam H. and Tom J.

Guarding With A Cold

MICKEY H. - It seemed that about every other summer I guarded, I would end up getting a head cold toward the end of the summer. It was probably from pushing myself too hard—partying all night and guarding all day. Guarding with a cold really got miserable on a brisk, windy day with warm water and rough surf. You'd see the tourists get in trouble and try to whistle them away from the rip, but eventually you had to get wet rescuing them. Then you'd have to sit there on the bench for the rest of the day shivering and miserable. It used to put me in a really bad mood.

A Surfer's Death

JACK C. - The saddest experience was when that surfer drowned. Joe and I worked on him for what seemed like an hour. The only way we could have saved his life was if we were standing on the sandbar and caught him before he fell. He swallowed so much water that there was nothing we could have done for him. Even if we had gotten him in, the water would have scarred his lungs, and he would have had emphysema. It changed my view of lifeguarding, and I realized how fragile life is. We were right there, and there was nothing we could have done for him.

To this day, we don't know if he had a seizure or hit his head because the autopsy was kept sealed—we know that a neck injury was ruled out. The family wanted it private. I saw marks on his head, so in my opinion, he hit his head, but I don't know.

I'm not going to judge what a surfer does or doesn't do, but the waves were crashing on the sandbar. It wasn't good surfing. We had a yellow (warning) flag up. We were trying to keep people in. It was sucking out and crashing on the sandbar.

Surfing in Lavallette is at your own risk.

Chug Contest

ANDY B. - Charlie B. was in a chugging contest with Patty K.'s friend. The first round was a draw. Charlie won the second one out-right. The guy said, "Let's do the best of three." He got halfway through and retched in the sink. Bob J. said to Patty, "Where did you find this gladiator?"

Observations Of A Mother Looking For A Child

GORDON H. - A mother looking for her lost child can be spotted from one thousand feet away. Many times I saw women looking for their children. Whether from fifty feet or a quarter mile, they stood out from the hundreds of people on the beach. Their strong, stiff-legged stride, with head darting from side to side, and long, intense glances to the water made them prominent from the clusters of other beachgoers. Their eyes were like darts thrown with fear. You could see in their faces that they were certain that the child, upon getting lost, was immediately swallowed up by the sea like a cat upon an unsuspecting mouse.

Blowin' In The Wind

GORDON H. - A child who loses his bearings almost always travels in the direction of the wind. At the beach, this narrows down the search possibilities when one is reported missing. Parents always seemed to worry that the sea swallowed up their child, but I never knew of a lost child even going in the water once they were lost. In many cases, though, the so-called "lost child" had gone back to the family's rented house without telling anyone.

Lost Children Have Changed

JACK C. - Today, the lost kids will not come with the lifeguard. They'll tell you, "I'm not going with you. My mommy told me not to go with strangers." And the kid's doing the right thing, but it's gotten crazy. You can't remove a splinter. This is insane.

On The Job Goofing

JIMMY A. ('66-'67) - There were slow days when the water was calm and you'd tell your partner, "I'll go play." You'd jump off the stand and deliberately trip over the rope box; you'd grab the rope to the torpedo buoy and get it tangled around your foot; you'd hit the water, and the buoy goes floating away because you didn't clip it, then you'd swim all the way out and have to swim back to the buoy. All that kind of stuff. And people would sit there on the beach watching this, thinking, "Is he serious?" And the rookie would say, "He's the senior lifeguard. He's really good. He's breaking me in."

Spear Gun

RAY B. ('55-'60) - We would take two spear guns out in the boat. The guy in the boat would load one while Jackie H. hunted with the other. When he hit something, he would hand the spear gun to the guy in the boat and grab the other spear gun. Once he nailed a drumfish. The guy in the boat reeled it in and half of it had been bitten off. From the arc of the bite, you knew it had to have been a shark. Nobody saw a shark.

August 14, 1967 - Captain's Notice #9

Try—and I know it is hard at times—but you are servants of the public. I received a few complaints about guards mouthing off at innocent people who were just up to tell you how to run the beach. Please answer them softly and try, even though it hurts, to do as they ask.

Boredom Fighters

JON S. - John T. would get bored, and he'd let people get in runs so he'd have something to do. "That person's getting close, should I whistle?" "Nah, let'm go, and we'll have something to do."

Fear Transmission

RANDY S. ('60s) - After I had been guarding for about five years, on really calm days I might take a late afternoon head break and puff on a roach. I'd return to the stand and choose to imagine myself as the Fun Supervisor. I'd groove on the immensity of the ocean, the communion people were having with nature, and the delight of children as they made their sand castles and ran from the waves. I don't believe my abilities to watch carefully or be ready in an emergency were ever compromised by getting high.

Once, though, when my bench partner went on his own head break,

I was getting into being very mellow and attentive when a youngster was brought up to the stand with a barbed fishhook curving through the palm of his hand. It really brought me down, and I focused on my role. I reassured the little guy down—he was probably about six or seven—and he was remarkably calm. Calm for several minutes, that is, until his mother got wind of the problem and approached the cluster of people that always seemed to gather when there was blood.

"Oh my God, what has happened?!" she shrieked, telegraphing tremendous fear to the boy. Immediately, the composure I had worked to build was shattered, and he began to cry. She completely lost sight of her role: to keep her son calm, quell his fears, and wait for a police car to take him to the doctor's where they would cut the barb off and remove the wire.

We Were Getting Hammered

JACK C. - In '95, Len H. and myself would time ourselves going out through some rough surf. It was taking us five to seven minutes to get out. We were getting hammered. We couldn't even let the bathers out to where they could get sucked in. If that happened, you couldn't get to them in time. You'd put your head up and a wave would break. You'd go under and you'd get pushed down—you'd get up—we were just trying to get out. The waves were unrideable. The scary part was that—God forbid if anything happened—you were walking on eggshells all day.

A Lousy Rescue

SAM H. ('62-'68) - I had another rescue that was lousy. I was with Ritchie A. It was sort of my fault. It was hot, and I had gone into the water for a dip, but I didn't take a can like they do now, which I think is a great idea. I got out there on the sandbar and the water got a little higher. All of a sudden, there was this girl who started moving and I said, "Are you alright?" And she said, "Yeah." I said, "That's alright,

I'll grab a hold of you," and then another girl went zipping by, so I had to get her too. Now I'm in the run, and we got into the area where the big waves are coming in, and I waved to Ritchie to come out. He was smart enough to come out with the rope. When he got there, I said, "Do you want me to put the belt on?" (I was a lot bigger than him.) But he said no, he was okay. I told him to lift the belt up, and we grabbed onto the can.

The people on the beach started pulling too fast, and with the current moving out, the water was just pouring over his head. Ritchie yelled, "Make them stop!" It was just streaming over his face. I was trying to signal the people on the beach to stop. So I let him go, and they pulled him right to shore. When he got in, he told the people not to pull so fast, just pull slow. Meanwhile, I'm going out again, so he had to swim out all over again. That was no walk in the park.

Double Death On The Rocks

JIM SIM ('63-'77) - Our big problems were from the jetties—they added to our problems. In Long Branch, they are all different lengths and placed at irregular intervals. We lost two people at one time on the jetties. They were on some kind of floatation devices—tubes or rafts. They started to drift out on a run. If they had continued out, they would have gone past the jetties and been safe. But they went toward the jetties and the waves pushed them into the rocks. One had his head smashed into the rocks and died. The other got a leg lodged in the rocks and drowned.

Saved By The Captain

BOBBI A. ('65-'69) - We were at a party. Either at John T.'s or the Stake Out. Patty and I jumped over the fence of the Candlelight Motel and went swimming with Jake and Sam. Of course, we had had a couple of drinks. The night watchman called the police. Dick G., the captain, was waiting across the street in his car, and he took us away, soaking and dripping wet. Dick was at the party and knew what we were going to do. He covered for us. Jake and Sam got caught, though. They ended up getting reprimanded—either they got docked pay or got sent to the bay. Jake got really angry—'cause we got away with it.

Torn Treads

GORDON H. - By the end of the summer, my swollen feet were marked by the jagged runes of nicks, gouges, punctures, and high impact collisions—a really ugly wreck. Splinters, fine glass shards, and shells caused accumulated damage despite the thick calluses you developed from walking through the hot sand and on blistering pavement.

One night after a few drinks, a girlfriend and I got tipsy and decided to run through yards of clotheslines and go towel snatching. At almost a full gallop, I hit a cinderblock outcropping, ending what had been a promising career in petty larceny. Biting into a red and blue towel I had just snatched, in midnight pain, I mutely waltzed and skipped several hundred feet to the sanctuary of my Volkswagen.

There is no way to dress a cut so that it will stay free of sand when you work on the beach.

Carrying The Can

JOE S. - With the cans, how that started... I had guarded at Seaside for one year, and they never left the stand without the can. They taught me that "the can is your lifeline." I used to see other guards leave the stand without cans. Jimmy used to joke and say, "You're a candy-ass taking your can." When I became lieutenant, I recommended the guards always take the cans whenever they leave the stand—even if it is just to walk over and talk to someone. If you notice—even today— they continue to carry the torpedo buoys when they get off the bench. I'm proud that I convinced them to make it part of their procedures.

Party Places

JOHN V. ('66-'70) - We had baseball games against the beach crew and the boro workers. It was an excuse to have another party after the game. When there was no house to hold the party, we held them under the West Point Island Bridge. Then I was at one of those parties on Mosquito Island. I got stranded and had to swim back. Gerry J., the policeman, picked me up walking along Bay Boulevard and gave me a lift home. It was the last time I drank gin.

Innocence Lost

EDWARDO B. - I never had been laid. Charlie said he'd have to do something about that. Charlie called a girl over—it might have been his girlfriend—and said, "Take care of my friend." That was it, my first time. I didn't know what I was doing, but I lost my virginity.

Solo Surfboating

GORDON H. - The Surf Club had a fiberglass Van Dyne surfboat. It was lightweight, and one man could easily row it except in rough surf. When the waves and tide were right at slow times, Pete would take the boat out and ride waves by himself. Once he caught a wave, he would scoot to the stern with the tiller oar and steer the boat toward shore. On a really good ride, he would toss the tiller up in the air, spin himself around, and catch it before it fell overboard.

August 20, 1967 - Captain's Notice #10

Guards - From now on I want one mother (guard)
on the beach at all times, not a beach cop.
If you want to play in the bathtubs, take one
from each beach. Today all beaches had tourists
in between 3:00 and 4:30 and Beaches
1-3-4 had no others to watch the sports. Beach 5
took their tub out but left one man behind to
watch the sports. Beach 2 also left one man
behind. Thanks to our lieutenant.

After patting Beach 5 on the back, I go up there
and what do I see? Four snappers around the
stand and one sliding pond expert putting
sand on the surfboard and showing the
snappers how he can slide the length of
the board with just a short run. I'm sure this
sport would be much better in a bedroom:
run, slide, and pole vault right into bed.

Fouled Rescue

GORDON H. - One day at the Surf Club, we had a strong undertow directly in front of the lifeguard stand. We kept everyone close to shore and tried to keep them to either side of the run. We knew there was a good possibility that we would have a rescue before the day was over. Sure enough, about 11:00 a.m. three boys with some kind of flimsy balloon floating device got in the seapuss and began to move away from the shoreline.

My partner, Smitty, was the first in the water with a free can. Before he got to them, I threw the line loop over my shoulder and headed out to link with him. Swimming in the run, we were going with the strong flow. It took me a little bit longer to reach them because the drag on the line slowed me down.

When I got to them, Smitty was reassuring the little boys that everything was okay, that they did not have to worry, and that we'd be on shore in just a minute or two. I coiled my hand in the line to pull it toward Smitty and clipped it on the torpedo buoy, but the people on the shore began to pull on the line before I could get my hand out of the loop in the line. I was short of breath from the swim and did not have much air in my lungs when a large wave washed the victims and Smitty over me. My fouled hand held me under everyone, and I quickly panicked. A guard from an adjacent beach had joined to assist, so the nylon line now had the weight of two large men and three boys being pulled in at the same time. Two fingers of my hand were getting squeezed together as the people on the beach were unwittingly trapping me underwater. I managed to break to the surf just long enough to get a short breath and yell that I was fouled in the line. Then I was washed under again. Without a knife, the only option seemed to be to snap my fingers off when I ran out of air. My heart was pounding. Finally, after what seemed like ages of struggling to pull slack into the line with my one free hand, while running out of breath, the people on the shore stopped pulling long enough for me to free my hand.

When we got to shore, the flesh around my fingers was nearly cut to the bone. It was six months before I had any feeling in those fingers.

The Thalidomide Girl

GORDON H. - One Sunday, a person on the beach came up to me on the bench and said there was a little girl crying nearby. She seemed to be lost, and he thought there might be something wrong with her.

He led me to a two-year old girl. She had a precious face with lightly curled blond hair and blue eyes. She had the bewildered "nothing looks familiar to me—I'm lost" stance. I spoke to her with reassuring words. As her crying subsided, I reached for her hand. When I looked, I immediately withdrew my hand, shocked: she only had the thumb and pinky fingers on each hand. Her feet lacked the corresponding toes. Timidly, I guided her with my hand to her back. When we got to the stand, I handed her up to my partner and climbed up. As I held her high, my partner blew the whistle to gain the attention of the entire beach. Within moments, her mother came running up, embraced this sweet, misfortunate child, and left me with a haunting memory.

Body Surfing On The Big Days

MIKE H. ('39-'41, '46-'54) - One of the best memories I have of all the summers I spent on the Jersey Shore was bodysurfing on the really big hurricane swells. Often they would come in on clear, sunny days in late August when the water was the warmest. Almost always they would be closeouts, but I loved taking the drop before they exploded on the sandbar. Sometimes I had to go out alone because I could not talk anyone into going out with me.

Being used to surfing large swells came in handy when I went to Hawaii with my son in December 1966. We went over to Makaha one day when the locals were calling it a fifteen-to eighteen-foot surf. The waves were breaking over a quarter mile from the beach. My son was riding on his surfboard, and I was bodysurfing with an old Hawaiian fellow. I only got three waves that day, but they were probably the best of my life. There was so much bounce as you went down the face of them, it felt like someone was slapping you in the stomach. We were able to ride them from all the way outside to the beach.

Guard Party Rip-Off

ANDY B. - We had our fourth and final guard party a week before Labor Day. Steve G. and I were in charge of arranging the goddamn party. It was a real pain in the ass, let me tell you. Steve didn't help worth shit. None of the guys got their money in until the last minute.

My friend Bob had to buy the beer for us. To break even, I had to invite my friends George, Rico, and a few others. On my day off, I had to go running from beach to beach collecting money and making arrangements. I didn't have enough boats. I had to make hamburgers for everyone and had to use my own tubs and grills. At the party, I saw kids that didn't pay their $3.00. I was furious, but I was too drunk to do anything about it. The final insult was when I went to clean up after the party. It had been raided. One of the kegs was missing and all the things I had brought—my tub, two grills, the food, cups—were stolen. That morning, Tom J.—who never paid his $3.00—came up to me and complained that he had lost his parka. He wanted me to pay for it. I was so mad that I wanted to kill him. I told him to go to hell. Nobody even said thank you. And nobody lifted a finger to help. I lost sleep over it and hardly ate. I get mad right now thinking about it.

August 28, 1967 - Captain's Notice #11

Guards - From now on, please don't go in the water with your belt on unless you are going in on a pull. We would like to soften the belts before we put them away. Oil them every day.

NO BOATS will go in the water until the work is finished.

Walking Off The Job

GORDON H. - The summer I worked at the Surf Club was incredible. I'd guard six days a week and bartend on the weekends. I had never had such a successful social life. I worked with two guards who really made the job a lot of fun and one who didn't. The first two,

Smitty, a tight end for West Virginia—a big guy, and the other, Pete, a weekend guard that was a law student, were tops. The last one, Jim D., was a total jerk. He was the captain. It wasn't until the very end of the summer that we learned how big a jerk and how bad a lifeguard he was. That's when we went after several people on a pull. Smitty and I went out right away and got to the people. We were in a run, so we signaled for the line and waited. And waited. The captain stood on the stand and was too chickenshit to swim out the line. The son-of-a-bitch could barely swim! We had doubts about him 'cause he never went out in the deep water, but this confirmed it.

He did eventually come out with the line, and we made it back to shore. Smitty went up to the bar to change into a dry suit and get lunch. I was still steaming about Jim D.'s hesitancy to swim out the line. (Especially since two months earlier, during a lifeguard test, he had held the line tight while I had to swim it out, making it unnecessarily difficult.) When he got back up on the stand, he started off with something like, "The next time something like that happens..." He was about to make some excuse about how *we* shouldn't make *him* look bad. That did it for me. I don't know what I said, but he told me, if I didn't like it, I could leave the beach. I said, "Fine," and walked up to gather my gear. Smitty stopped me when I was approaching the snack bar and said, "What's happening?" I told him I had quit because Jim D. was making excuses for his piss-poor performance. Smitty walked down and began talking to Jim D. Almost immediately, I saw Smitty square off. He was getting intense. Then he came walking back: he quit too.

We had hoped that the owner would take this as a wake-up call that he had an incompetent running his beach, but he didn't. The owner was somewhere in La-La Land with his blazer and ascot. Anyway, later that day, Smitty and I went out, bought giant steaks and a couple of six-packs, and had a two-man party. We had had a tremendous summer up to that point, bartending, bouncing, and hustling almost every night.

A few weeks later, I hitchhiked to California and boarded a plane for Hawaii.

Female ocean lifeguards launch a Hankins surfboat in preparation for tournament competitions, circa 1997.

September

Light Changes

*O*nce August has passed, there is a melancholy that seems to ride on the very rays of light that reach the shore. The dry breezes have a bittersweetness to them, and the evenings are tinged with the stronger chills that are to come.

The waning days of the season are like a death knell for summer and the youth, hope, and carefree living that are a part of it. People's minds begin to drift toward more purposeful pursuits—college, school, business, and their homes. Romances either come to an end as the distance between lovers works a wedge between emotions, or they become deeper, stronger, and more mature.

The days immediately before and during the Labor Day holiday are legendary for lifeguards. Hurricanes and tropical storms, hundreds of miles away, seem to stir the piss-warm waters into torrents with forces like raging, flooding rivers. There is a tradition that the roughest, most rapidly changing surf is likely to occur on the last heavenly days that summer can bring forth. Over a ten-year period, the number *of rescues on the Labor Day weekend markedly increased during seven of them.*

One moment, bathers are in rapid currents around their knees; the next, they may find themselves chest deep in rushing water too power-ful to stand in. Even the fittest, fastest swimmers are overwhelmed by the force of the volume of water in the large waves that add to the shoreline currents. In an instant, large groups of people—five, ten, fifteen—have been put in peril as they were lifted off sandbars and car-ried to deeper water. It is under these circumstances that some of the greatest and most cursed rescues have occurred.

When old guards get together, Labor Day is spoken about with the reverence, awe, and nostalgia of a benediction for summer and life.

♠ ♠ ♠

Two Sides To A Stroke

JACK C. ('77-present) - At Midway [Beach], you had to swim to two buoys a day. You also had to paddle out and run a mile every morn-ing. One day in Lavallette, there had to be ten people in the water, and I was swimming from one buoy to the other, and my partner was on the stand. I was practicing bi-lateral breathing, so I never lost sight of the people in the water. There was nothing going on that day. I was swim-ming for about twenty minutes, and the captain came down to the stand and told me I had to stop. He was my boss, and I was eighteen, so I stopped, but I thought that was the stupidest thing I've ever heard.

Labor Day Was A Horror Show

ANDY B. ('65-'70) - I was working with Joe S. on Beach #8—of all the fucking places. It was about as rough as I have ever seen it while on duty. All day long we were on our toes, trying to keep people from going out past the drop, that's how bad it was.

By 5:30 p.m., it was dead high tide, and I've never seen anything like it. We had moved the boat back to the boardwalk to turn it over, and the stand was buried by now. The ocean was a bubbling cauldron—"pure violence" would be the only way to describe it. There were only two bathers left. Joe and I were breathing easy for the first time.

With absolutely no warning, one of the stupid bathers got caught. Joe and I had figured out in advance what we would do. I'd go with the can, and he'd follow with the line. One problem though: there was no one around to help pull the line in. Not having time to debate the matter, Joe called up Bill for help as I was entering the water.

My feeling about the situation was very simple: I was terrified. The waves tossed me like I was a toy. I felt so small and mortal. I can't describe the feeling. The adrenalin was shooting through me, and I must have possessed inhuman energy for at least ten minutes. Even though the waves were pushing hard against me and tossing me everywhere, I made it to my victim in less than two minutes—a one hundred fifty-yard swim. It seems that I just became part of the huge undertow.

Anyway, I reached my victim, a grown man, offered him the can, and talked and talked, trying to reassure him. After about five minutes, I realized Joe was not going to make it. (I found out later that one of the tourists grabbed his line and pulled him back, sending him simultaneously into a rage and panic.)

Seeing as we were getting battered by waves that began breaking a half mile out and getting extremely frightened, I decided to come in alone. We were off of Elizabeth Avenue—four blocks down from where I entered the water—and out of the undertow so that the waves were pushing us in. They were also drowning us. On one wave I lost the poor guy. While probing with my feet, I hit him in the face. I pulled him up by the hair and draped him over the can. This time, I got him in a full-nelson and held him on the can. This put his back to the waves and made the two of us inseparable. If he were to drown, at least I wouldn't have the shame of coming in alone. Since we were above water, the waves were killing us, but at least we got in faster. Joe and

Hoffman came in to help us out.

That damn guy I rescued was so tired that he collapsed on the beach and lay there for five minutes before he moved. I did the same. Joe felt so bad, he was almost crying. I felt boundless pity for Old Joe. That night, I passed out at 11:00 without drinking. That one day made the whole summer.

The Big Pull

JOE S. ('68-'76, '90s, '00s) - I remember it clearly. It was 5:30 in the afternoon. We had had some pulls earlier in the day, and we were getting ready to close down by 6:00. We had already moved the boat back away from the water. Then this woman started yelling for her husband. He was right next to the shorebreak when he got caught in the undertow. We saw him going out. Andy was off right away with a can. Andy got in the rip and shot out like a bullet. I said, "Holy shit!"

I can remember taking the phone off the hook so they would know at headquarters that no one was on the beach. I jumped into the rip. Right after I left, I remember hearing the crack. The rope box must have been dragged into the water, and it must have snapped when a wave hit it. The other end of the line was now loose and dangling. Andy and I knew we were in big trouble then. I continued to try to swim out, then people on the beach started to pull in on the line, and I couldn't get to Andy. I didn't know what was going on—I figured the rope was tangled. I almost disconnected the line. I could see Andy with the torp, but I couldn't see the victim. When I finally got there, the guy was real bad—his lips were really blue. Andy was okay, but after we got hit by four or five waves together, his back was to the guy, and I was facing the waves. The white water was holding us down. You wouldn't think that the waves would be breaking that far out, but they kept breaking. It was so massive. The rip was so bad. I thought with the waves breaking that there was a sandbar and we could hit bottom, but we couldn't. The waves were breaking one right after another. We kept trying to reach bottom to kick ourselves up, but we couldn't reach it. We were under the water a long time.

I kept thinking, "If we don't get up, this guy is going to die on us."

Meanwhile, the woman had picked up the lifeguards' phone and told the dispatcher, "My husband and two lifeguards just drowned." She couldn't see us—we were too far out and were hidden by the waves. Dick Hoffman, the captain of the guards, took a patrol car from headquarters down the one-way highway the wrong way with Ted G., one of the summer police officers.

A U.S. Coast Guard helicopter was sent to look for us.

It was at this point that we broke out of the rip. We were out such a distance that the water calmed down a bit. That's when we started to swim in.

We saw boats starting to go out. We went from Trenton Avenue all the way over to Elizabeth Avenue—nearly four blocks. From when this whole thing started, and Andy got to the guy, and I got to him, was probably about fifteen minutes.

When we got close to the beach, the other guards helped us in. On the beach, that's when everybody there was thinking, "Holy cow, how did this thing happen?"

It was about 6:10 or 6:20 when this whole thing was over. It was at the line box that people were panicking. They were holding onto the line thinking they were helping me. It was so far out that it ran the whole length of line out—more than one thousand feet of line.

The victim was stabilized, but they probably took him to the hospital just to check him out. But he was in bad shape. If it wasn't for Andy, we would never have gotten that guy. Andy's speed and reaction made the difference. He was the fastest swimmer, and I was the strongest swimmer with the rope. It was teamwork. It was the type of day we were thankful that we were together. With a weak guard, something would have happened, and it wouldn't have been pleasant.

We were in the water so much that day that our skin was white from the salt in the water.

♠ ♠ ♠

The Big Rescue - Part I: Paybacks

ANDY B. - As the blinding heat of late August gives way to the mild tropical breezes of September, the usually tranquil New Jersey surf heats up in rushing currents, churned and antagonized by huge, beautifully shaped waves crashing in watery avalanches a quarter mile or more from shore. Often a season punctuated by several lost children, a surfboard or two in the face, a rescue or two in the "wash," or a geriatric heart seizure in a freezing cold surf, could end in a flurry of dramatic and often life-threatening multiple rescues. The rescues involved boats, surfboards, rescue cans, and a tangle of rescue lines amidst the terrible pleas and screams of bathers flailing desperately as they were swept hopelessly further to sea.

Guards, and even veterans, who have spent the preceding ten weeks gabbing away during boring afternoons bundled against the relentless damp of the southeast wind while surreptitiously sipping coolers of vodka and Gatorade, would suddenly find themselves in the center of a firestorm. Then they would be forced to think with their nerves, never aware at the time that with one small error in their unthinking, physical judgment, their actions could result in a sudden loss of life, perhaps even their own.

It was on one such violent Labor Day that I set up shop on the southernmost beach in Lavallette with my portly bench partner, Charlie. Charlie, in addition to being a less-than-perfect physical specimen, also suffered from terrible vision. He wore the proverbial "Coke bottle-thick" eyeglass lenses. He also suffered from an inordinate love of the good life, an affliction which we shared. Such were our respective reputations that our captain thought it fitting that we deserved each other, and since we were such good friends, we should not afflict other guards. Besides, I think he reasoned it was easier to keep tabs on the two malcontent troublemakers if they were concentrated in one locale.

On this particular Labor Day, both of us had been out late the previous night and were still recovering as the afternoon wore on. The events of that morning had been ominous. The abating tide, as it so often does, caused ripping currents with two rescues, one of them a close call where Charlie, half-blind, had to dive in an effort to find an exhausted and submerged girl as she was dragged under and away from the shore by the river-like rip current. Groping desperately, his hand eventually hit her head, and he immediately dragged her to the surface and the shore. After bringing up her ration of seawater and getting oxygen, she was reunited with her parents, presumably never to go near saltwater again.

By the afternoon, we both shared her fear. As noon's dead low tide changed to high tide in mid-afternoon, the larger waves again rekindled: large, violent waves crashed into an ever-steepening seawall bringing terrible rip currents, which selectively sought valleys and gullies in the sandbar to rush back out to sea.

Shortly after 3:00 p.m., right after Charlie returned from a head break where he drank nearly a quart of orange juice to get more vitamin C in his alcohol-saturated body, a tremendous set of waves came in, leaving bathers diving for the bottom or foolishly hanging onto the boundary ropes. As the last waves rolled in, we began to see a wide swath of ripples forming over nearly the entire beach, indicating, quite simply, a river running straight out to the shipping lanes. Then we began to see it, first on the face of one bather, then another, and then a dozen or more: the look of desperation as they attempted to lamely stroke for the beach and into the teeth of this five mile per hour river. I heard my partner mumble, "Oh, Jesus Christ." Without really thinking, I clipped a rescue can onto my belt, quickly instructed Charlie to call Bill, the dispatcher, at the shack for back-up help, and to follow me out with a line. After I ran toward the water and entered the surf at a sprint,

I was shocked at how quickly the current carried me to the disaster area. Almost magically, within ten strokes, I was in the midst of a screaming, panicking cluster of victims, grabbing frantically at both myself and the symbolic salvation of the red and white rescue torp. In an instant, like a magnet attracting metal fragments, a half-dozen bathers were clinging to me for dear life. As I looked back, I saw blind Charlie with a rescue can but no line, suffering the same predicament. As the two of us drifted out with our respective burdens, a guard from the next town over, Ortley Beach, reached us with a line, enabling us to unload our bathers; we instructed them to hold onto the line. As we looked around, we saw other guards—some with buoys, others swimming out lines—picking up clusters of would-be drowning victims and putting them onto the lines. They were then being pulled toward the beach by makeshift groups of volunteers being instructed by other guards and beach police. I later learned that one creative guard had swum in a giant, semi-circular arc around the entire beach with a rescue line trailing behind, thus allowing volunteers at either end of the line on opposite sides of the beach to pull the line in like a giant seining net, catching drowning bathers as well as exhausted guards. Guards came from as far as a three-quarter mile radius, some by bicycle on the boardwalk, some sprinting down the beach, and some even speeding by automobile.

Somewhere outside all this bedlam, I drifted. After dragging several batches of victims to the rescue lines, which by now were tangled, I surrendered my torpedo buoy, laden with bathers, to another faceless guard. This enabled me to set out after one lone bather whom I had spotted bobbing up and down between the waves beyond the breakers and waving one arm while trying desperately to stay afloat with the other. I got to him soon enough; both of us were exhausted. Few words were exchanged as I tried to kick and tread water while holding him with one arm and waving for help with the other. I remember him starting to cry, and I knew it would be only a minute or two before my own exhausted carcass would slip below the surface.

And then a mirage appeared. Our surfboat, operated by a middle-aged man and a skinny youth of about my own age, had somehow made it through the maelstrom without being capsized or swamped. (It would be only a few years later that I would again meet the skinny youth in my work place, when, one afternoon, I listened in shock as he recounted the Labor Day afternoon on Beach #6 when he and his father almost got themselves killed trying to help out in a massive rescue.) My surprise at seeing a surfboat in a near-hurricane surf being manned by two civilians was quickly overcome by gratitude as I paddled over to the transom, and with one last, great heave, pushed my victim over the transom by the ass of his pants so that he was draped headfirst into the stern of the boat. I then started pulling myself over the transom in hopes of getting the boat back to the beach somehow, but stopped instantly and hung suspended in a chin-up position while I watched in horror as a monster swell blotted out the eastern sky. Almost simultaneously, the nose of our would-be rescue boat began to drift to my left.

"Left oar, hit the left oar!" I remember screaming hoarsely. "A wave's coming!"

Our heroes reacted quickly—too quickly—as they immediately fouled each others left oars. One of them popped his out of the oarlock while the other hit his oar too hard and it skidded ineffectively over the water's surface.

We would have just cleared this monster wave if the vessel had been squared and two or three hard, biting strokes followed. As it was, the boat was at a nearly forty-five degree angle as the rooster comb engulfed the boat.

I dove for the bottom just before it would have hit me in the face. I lingered for a long moment beneath the churning explosion, being tossed about. When I bobbed back to the surface, I saw a soup containing the overturned boat, a collection of oars, and a half dozen or so bodies now being shoved toward the beach by the force of the monster wave. We were no longer a quarter mile offshore. With the same power with which we had been dragged out, we were now being pushed back in.

Rip currents are a phenomenon in New Jersey and elsewhere. Bathers are invariably drawn away from the beach and subsequently dragged by the prevailing drift, usually northward in a semi-circular arc and deposited back on the beach. The trick is to not fight the current, but to either just go with it or swim to the side of it. Unless the surf is of hurricane proportions, survival depends on the simple ability to stay calm and keep treading water. Most bathers don't know this. Lifeguards, or at least the experienced ones, do.

Thus it was that the lot of us were now being boomeranged toward shore by this force of nature. I looked for the body of my victim; his head was down, and I lifted it from the water by his hair. He was semi-conscious but was still spitting water. I took him in a cross-chest carry and kicked maybe thirty yards before willing hands waded out, relieved me of my burden, and dragged me to a blanket.

The scene on the beach was bedlam: police cars arrived bearing badly needed oxygen tanks, and ambulances responded to first aid sirens. People everywhere were sprawled out and wrapped up in blankets, being attended to by professionals and people on the scene.

It was here, still gasping for breath, that I ran into Charlie, who moments before was puking the orange juice he had drunk minutes before the big rescue.

"Nice mess you created here, asshole," he said. "Do you know what the estimate on the number of saves is?"

"About thirty, maybe forty, I would guess," I replied.

"Try between sixty and one hundred. Every beach except Beach #1 and #2 came to help, plus several of Ortley's beaches."

"What happened to the line you were going to bring?" I asked.

"Had to unclip it. Some jerks on the beach started pulling me in before I even got close to you. It wouldn't have mattered anyway."

Miraculously, no one drowned or was even hospitalized. No traumatic memories in a day that was full of memorable moments.

The Big Rescue - Part II: Hangers On

CHARLIE B. ('65, '67-'71) - I'd like to match notes and see what I remember about the big rescue. We had a lot of rescues that day. We were almost always on the beach instead of the stand because we were so busy. It was at the beach where the "renters" lived—people who came down for the week, so they didn't know much about the water. Andy took the torp; I took the rope. The current was sweeping northbound. I went forty yards up the beach hoping to sweep around the people who were all washing in that direction and to ring them in. As I swam out, though, the people in close grabbed the rope, and I couldn't pull it out anymore. I was going nowhere. I told them to let it go, but they didn't want to.

By now, Andy had about three or four people on his torp. I unhitched the line and gave away my torp.

That was when I saw the lifeboat coming out. Some people on the beach—I think there were three—launched the surfboat. When they got out where I was, I yelled, "What are you doing with the boat?" They didn't know what they were doing. Then they turned the boat parallel to the beach to pick someone up and got broadsided by a wave. They flipped the boat. People hung onto the side.

Eventually, the twenty or thirty people who got swept along ended up at the end or edge of the strong current. Then it seemed that the water just stopped. I'd say I was out in the water about half an hour.

The Big Rescue - Part III: All Together Now

ANDY B. - The most exciting part of the season came after my regular bench partner had returned to college. On the day before Labor Day, there was a total of seventy-five pulls on the six beaches. Charlie and I pulled out thirty-five on Beach #6. In a period of fifteen minutes, thirty people got caught in a run on our beach. It took six guards, a boat, and help from the people on the beach before we got everyone out. Sam H. and Rich A. ran down from Beach #5; John Shawn and Marty G. came from Beach #4. Marty drove down in his car. That's Marty all the way.

The Big Rescue - Part IV: Swamped Rescue

SAM H. ('62-'68) - I only remember a few rescues. We were working on Beach #5. It was one of those Labor Day weekends. The runs were really moving—they were going out about a quarter mile. And the waves were just monstrous, closing out; they were crashing.

So we took off and ran down the beach: it took us about five or six minutes to row that block, and then a wave hit us. By the time we got down to Beach #6, we had a boat half filled with water. There had to be fifty people in this pull—it was monstrous, it was *monstrous*. So all these people are holding onto the boat, so we put the bow into the waves, and we were going in. We told the people "Just hold on, and when the wave comes, it's going to go, so you just come back to it." We couldn't do anything with it cause it was half full of water. Then it rolled, and we rolled, and then the people were holding onto the boat, and we just started to yank the people in. They were just holding onto the sides of the overturned boat. There was nothing we could do with it. The waves were big—they had to be about six feet high. And they were just crashing and crashing, and it was a mess. We took the people back and forth.

The boat's over, we were stern first. There was nothing we could have done. You have all that water hitting you. You're rowing and rowing and you couldn't get anywhere, and the puke was coming up in your throat.

I'm heading out this one time, not too far from shore, and I came up through a wave, looked, and saw this guy looking at me. He was sinking. He looked like hell. I said, "I can't get you, somebody's right behind me. I got to get the furthest one."

When I got to the beach, that poor bastard, he was on the beach puking. He was blue. It was awful. It was scary. It was like an eruption. The water was so bad that we didn't even party hard that night 'cause we couldn't—we were too tired and nervous. That's how scary it was—and we were fearless.

The Big Rescue - Part V: Yelling And Screaming

JIMMY A. ('66-'67) - There were thirty-six people rescued. We were all probably up there—we had come down with the beach truck. We knew the south end of town had a bad problem. They were trying to keep the people in really close. We had all the weekenders that came in the south end of town. I was in the water. I think I took out the boat. It was nasty, nasty surf. Everybody was yelling, but nobody could hear each other. People were running everywhere. The people on the beach started to pull on the line before the lifeguard could get out to the furthest people. The people on the beach took out a boat, and I remember them capsizing it in the wash. There were boats that went in from another beach. It was people all over the place. You were focusing on everything. The one surfboat was loaded with water, and people were holding onto it. Everyone was yelling and screaming.

The Big Rescue - Part VI: A Victim's Point Of View

SHARON M. ('60s-present) - I was a victim in that big rescue. I was so embarrassed. These were the guys that I partied with, and I had to get pulled in along with everyone else.

* * *

Labor Day Rescue At The Surf Club

MIKE H. ('39-'41, '46-'54) - About 1975, we had a typical Labor Day: hot and sunny with warm water and a huge swell running. A bunch of people got caught in a rip in front of the Surf Club in Ortley Beach. Both guards went out to get them. Quite a few ex-guards were at the Surf Club celebrating Labor Day in typical lifeguard fashion— drinking heavily. They saw the two guards struggling with the people and decided to help. They grabbed another rope and torpedo and headed out.

By now, there were over a dozen people clustered in the rip, including guards and inebriated ex-guards. Everyone was shouting and giving directions, and no one knew who was in charge. Since the surf was big, it started washing everyone around. Before long, the two ropes had gotten wrapped around everyone, and it was one mass of people roped together getting hammered by the waves. People on the beach saw the loose ropes lying on the beach and started pulling on them to help, which served to pull people underwater.

All in all, it was not a life or death situation. The guards and ex-guards and other helpers had it somewhat under control. No one was going to drown, but they sure got bashed around and put on a great comedy show for the people on the beach. In fact, a number of people jumped in the water and let themselves get sucked out in the rip so they could be rescued. After a while, it seemed to turn into a Large Rescue/Labor Day Party in the water.

Blown Bulbs

RANDY S. ('60s) - Kirk, two other guards, and I went down to a bar on the boardwalk. We closed the place at 2:00 a.m. Needless to say, we were drunk on our asses. Crazy ass Kirk and I climbed up the Ferris wheel in Funtown and unscrewed light bulbs and started throwing them at the other guards. And damn if we didn't get put in jail. We got off pretty easy, though. We only had to pay $10.00 bail each, plus the cost of the bulbs. It was fun, though, and the bulbs made a sharp noise when they broke.

I also ran into a nymph! She was at a party, and she hustled me.

She wasn't real sharp, but she wasn't too bad, either. We just fucked for a whole week—what a way to end the summer.

Groupies vs. Girlfriends

HOBIE ('65-'74) - Girlfriends were usually treated differently than groupies. Girlfriends were usually treated with as much respect as possible by a bunch of young, horny guys. Groupies were a different story. Every year, there were several groupies that hung out with the squad. Usually, by the end of the summer, they had been enjoyed by at least several members of the squad. Most never lasted more than one summer.

Sometimes things could get a little out of hand. The last year I was allowed to guard in Lavallette, we pulled a couple of groupies into the shack on Labor Day and ripped all of their clothes off. The captain's ten-year old son was there and hanging from the rafters like a little monkey taking in the show. I am sure he had some great stories to tell his fourth grade friends.

No one tried to rape them or anything, just a little grabbing. They couldn't have minded it too much, because they could see that it was coming before it really started. Besides, one of them came back the next weekend for a repeat performance. I remember one of them saying to her girlfriend, "They think we are sluts." Her girlfriend replied, "Well, what do you expect?"

Trade-Offs

JACK C. – It's a lifestyle of little means, but it's a lifestyle I wouldn't trade for anything. I chose it, and it worked out for me.

We had a guard—she was looking forward to going back to school. She was having a rough summer. I don't want to get into it—she was seeing a guard on the beach, and he dumped her. You know the whole thing. It kinda looked bad. And she goes, "I kinda can't wait to get back to school." And I said, "Ya know what? Your best day at school isn't better than your worst day up here on the beach."

The End

CHARLIE B. - I was considered the culprit. I was from out of town—taking all the fair-haired local boys and corrupting them. There were a lot of guards that weren't allowed to go to The Cave. I don't think we were sober for two months. We were bad.

In the end, I can't remember whether I got fired or not. It was real "touch and go" there for a while. It seems to me I remember being told, "Andy's gonna stay, and you're not from town, so you're gonna go." They thought I was corrupting the innocent youth of Lavallette.

Peril Below

JOE S. - In September, when we were storing all the gear for the winter, John and I were diving to pull the anchors up that held the beach area ropes. John reached down and got a fishhook in his hand underwater. We couldn't get it out. We ended up ripping the hand with the hook backwards.

The Lightness Of Being

MICHELLE P. ('77-'80, '83-'84) - I remember Cres calling once and docking me for sea glass hunting while on duty. I remember jogging on the boardwalk at 5:00 a.m. and watching the seagulls. I remember flying a kite from the stand one whole day. I remember handing out band-aids and telling the time endlessly. I remember dragging the stand up at the end of the day and having an utter feeling of great calm.

The Whale's Tale

MICKEY H. ('67-'76) - The last summer I was guarding, we actually spotted a whale about one hundred-fifty yards off the beach. Of course we all raced to the boat to check it out. We were able to get really close to it, so when it raised its tail to dive, we were actually looking up at its flukes. I was amazed at how gentle he was. It seemed like he was moving in slow motion, yet you could see the power. After rowing around him for about ten minutes with some boats from other beaches, I felt that I had to do something to liven up their day. So we rowed real close, and I dove over the side and tried to grab onto the whale's tail. Looking back, it is just as well that I didn't grab it. If he freaked out, he could have crushed me like an ant.

Shortly after that, he made a deep dive and disappeared. This was the one and only live whale that I have ever seen off the Jersey coast. Being out there with him was one of the highlights of the years I spent on the bench.

Off Season

BUTCH S. (mid-'60s) - We met two girls at the end of the season. They came down again one weekend, and Hobie and I had them rent a motel room. I didn't pick up Toni until 11:00 p.m. because she worked late. Hobie went to the motel before I got there. Later, Toni and I went to the motel. When we got there, Hobie and Nancy were bareass in bed, so we took off our clothes and went to bed with them. There we were— all four of us— just fucking and fucking. It was really funny. I had never seen anyone screw before, and now I was close enough to pinch her on the ass. Hobie and I would grab each other's date's boobs and just break up laughing.

Then Hobie and Nancy went in and took a shower. I crept into the bathroom, stuck my hand into the shower and started to finger Nancy. She thought it was Hobie. She was just getting out of her mind. Hobie was snickering because he knew. After about six or seven minutes, I had to stop when she discovered what was going on. Then we got blowjobs. We were pretty worn out the next day.

First Timers

HOBIE - It always amazed me how you could meet a girl one afternoon and be her first lover that night, even though she might have a steady boyfriend or even a fiancé. This happened to me at least three times.

I would meet a girl, and that night, I would be the first man to have sex with her. Looking back, I feel a little guilty about it, but if their boyfriends were not man enough to do the job, I was young and horny and ready to take care of it. It still amazes me that they would be willing to do it with a lifeguard that they had just met instead of with their boyfriends.

A large number of the girls that guards were having sex with in the '60s and '70s were under the legal age of consent. Personally, when I was sober, I always tried to make sure that the girls I was with were at least sixteen, and even then I felt a little guilty if they were not at least eighteen. Some of the other guards, however, were not so particular. I remember one guard getting an award at a lifeguard banquet for having a date half his age. He was twenty-six and she was thirteen. As bad as I may have been at that time, I always felt that was wrong.

It often amazed me that with all of the sex that the guards were having, there was very little venereal disease. It may have been because a high percentage of the girls that were having their sex were first timers or had not had more than one or two partners before they got involved with us. Since many of the girls we were enjoying were away from home on vacation for a couple of weeks or the entire summer, they could go wild and not have to worry about their reputations at school. I know that at least a few of the groupies were the real clean-cut, captain-of-the-cheerleader-squad-types at their high school.

Some people may think that I was cold and callous, but I was young and felt that at least a part of my job was making sure that the tourist's daughters had a great vacation. Maybe we were using them, but a lot of times they were using us to fulfill a summer fantasy.

What Am I Doing Here?

JON S. ('66-'74) - I was married and living on West Point Island. We were closing the beach down, and Charley P. came up like a little kid. "You wouldn't believe what Adam and I have back at the Island House!" He had picked up this girl, shit-faced drunk, at a bar at about 4:00 in the morning in Manasquan and brought her back to the Island House they were renting. I drove the truck from the beach over with about seven people. We're all in bathing suits, and we go in and sit down. Here's this girl with a sheet over her—stark naked. And Charlie's like a little kid. They didn't do shit to the girl. They started shooting fireworks up the chimney to wake her up. Poor girl woke up, no clothes on, with seven guys just looking at her that she had never seen before. She didn't know where she was—she could have been in upstate New York; then I started to think, "*Hmmm*, I'm just married, maybe I shouldn't be here."

A Surfer With Too Many Victims

KENNY A. ('60s-'90s) - I was surfing with Tony. It was about two weeks after Labor Day in 1967. It was an Indian summer day. I was surfing with my friend. There were great sandbars. Since it was after the season, we drove our VW on the beach.

We saw a fire truck at the end of the street a few blocks down the beach and decided to see what was going on. When we got there, we saw that there was a man offshore in a boat who couldn't get in, and they were trying to figure what to do about it. But it wasn't like he was in any immediate danger, although the waves were really big.

So we turned around and drove a few blocks back when someone came running up and said a kid was drowning. I ran to the run and swam. I was amazed at how fast I got to him—it was a fast run. I told the kid—he was between eight and eleven years old —"Kid, hold on around my neck," I told him, "but don't choke me."

The next thing I know, I hear, "Help! Save me! Help!" It was someone else that got sucked into the run. Apparently, he came out to help, but got overwhelmed. We got to him and started in. Then it happened again: "Help! Help!" It was another man. As it turned out, it was the kid's father. We managed to link up. There were now four of us together. The waves were really big that day. Then it happened *again!* "Help, help me!"

I got over nearby, but I couldn't get to him. I tried to talk him in. I put all our lives back in jeopardy by going with the flow to where this guy was. My hand just barely grazed his, and he kept on going. I tried to talk him in.

"Float! Kick! Take a deep breath!" I said. "When you get to the breakers, I want you to go underneath and swim as fast as you can out to sea—you'll be all right."

"I can't, I can't!" he screamed.

I then said, *"I can't."* I just couldn't do anymore—I wasn't sure I was even going to survive, especially with that kid choking me.

We made it to the beach and collapsed. The chief of police came over, and I told him someone else had drowned, but he didn't believe me. I said, "There's another person in the water, and he has drowned. Get your search crew together. He'll probably wash up in that area."

He kept saying, "Are you sure? Are you sure?" I was so annoyed, I wanted to punch the bastard.

I said, "Yes, I am sure! He'll probably wash up over there, that's where the water's circling." Sure enough, twenty minutes later, we saw an arm flop over in the surf: it was the guy. He was only twenty-four years old and a fireman from Newark. He had rescued a lot of people, but he just didn't know the water.

In the days afterward, I was okay during the day, but at night, I had nightmares about it for months. Although I was never a paid lifeguard, I rescued a lot more that year—I looked around and spotted the people before they even knew they were in trouble. By the time I reached them, they knew they were in trouble. That's when they said, "Thank

God you got here."

That time with the boy and the three men was the one time I had a problem—*I couldn't see the problem developing.*

Five Drownings

JON S. - Sam H. got married on a Saturday in the fall while we went out body surfing off the end of the street here. A whole lot of people, all the old guards, had gathered on the beach. We were having a ball. No guards were there. Big waves were going right off the end of the jetty. It was like a big ski run. Just go right out, swim over, ride in, and go around in a big circle. That afternoon, I think five people drowned between here and Seaside Heights. There were no guards on duty—it was late September or early October of '69 or '70.

A window on the world. On calm days, the conversation and company of a good bench partner can make this one of the best jobs in the world, building friendships that last a lifetime.

Looking Back

Guarding Camaraderie

BOB G. ('63-'67, '69) - It was a different atmosphere. There was a party every night and a lot closer friendships. There were always the same five or six guys together at night.

Making The Transition

JIM C. ('67-present; Captain '81-present) - The beach started to evolve where tournaments became more important and being good swimmers and doing all these competitive things started to get priority with the kids. It was time for some changes. Things weren't getting accomplished, and it became a political thing.

So when we came in, I said we have to have a system—a captain, a lieutenant, and three sergeants. We had more of an organizational flow chart—it can't just be a captain and a lieutenant riding around trying to watch all these guys doing all these things. Then it got into being in tournaments and working out, coming in at 7:30 or 8:00 in the morning and putting the time in prior to working. Guys will still get out during the day and paddle, and we encourage them to use the rescue tools.

So I think that's when it started.

Lawyers On The Beach

JACK C. ('77-present) - In my opinion, the change was brought about by insurance regulations because of lawsuits and attorneys and everything; the property values and the rental costs have dictated the transformation of the beach to what it is today. With the drinking age going up and the age of the guards going down, the beach had to become more professional and team-oriented. The budgets were less— it was more of a shoestring operation back then. Now, you gotta have a guard for every one hundred feet of beach, you gotta have a back-board, we got a truck. We've got oxygen because there is an attorney looking over your shoulder.

JIM C. - Our attorney advised us in lieu of this Cape May case (because of the dunes blocking the view), that you *can* be held negligent or liable if you have lifeguards on duty on rainy days. They no longer stay in their cars at the top of the street where they can't see the beach. He has advised us that when you're on, you're on. So now, we have everyone stay at the shack when it rains. Now that most of the kids don't live in Lavallette, we keep them in the shack.

We have signs at the top of every street that say, "Lifeguards on duty 10:00 - 5:00." What he wanted us to do was cover them or put up different signs. So—quick thinking—we quickly pulled them off— twenty-eight streets in the rain—got a little stencil made up really fast, and spray painted, "No guards on duty. Beach closed." We flipped the signs over and screwed them in. Well, at two o'clock the sun came out, it was beautiful like this, and we went back out, flipped the signs over, screwed them back in, and they said, "Lifeguards on duty..." again.

Equipment Changes

JIM C. - The equipment has evolved from a metal can to the red-and-white cans, to the hard can, to the soft cans; the surfboards—

from nothing to a Charlie Keller board, to a Gordon and Smith-type board, to the marine rescue board, to the racing board. Rescues are still the same.

Changing Waters

JIM C. - I hate to be like the old timers, 'Well, you know, back in my day...,' but it seems like the water was rougher back then—it seemed like we had more rescues than we have today. We've had very few rescues this year. Maybe we've become more conscious of keeping people from getting in trouble. Remember, we used to have ropes in the water. There was a set area—people had to go in there. We just kinda boxed people in; now we're going from jetty to jetty (without roped-in bathing areas). We've got surfing areas, swimming areas, boogie board areas: it is still basically the same, but I think there's more people.

The water is different, the techniques are different—I think we are more preventative.

A Clean Job

RUSSELL F. ('50-'51) - As far as I can see, of all the summer jobs that people can have throughout the country, I think lifeguarding—no matter what beach it is on—is the cleanest, the best. It's a good education for children. It's a good way of life, a good way to start your career. It's a good background. It's not like working construction or with guys doing shots and beer.

Beyond The Bathers

MICKEY H. ('67-'76) - Sitting on the bench six days-a-week for nearly nine hours-a-day gave you a lot of time to look at the water. On an especially calm day, when there was little chance of anyone getting into trouble, your eyes would periodically look beyond the bathers out to the open ocean. In the ten summers I spent on the bench watching the water, I have probably seen more than most people, but it still amazes me how little sea life is evident off the Jersey coast. It could be for a lot reasons. The area right off the beach is like a desert: flat and sandy with little food and few places to hide.

Innocence Lost

ANDY B. ('65-'70) - Much is made of the glamorous nature of guarding. Now that the few precious seasons have long since slipped away and most of us have gone on to vocations which have us tied to a desk, cooped up away from the sun and fresh air and sweating the days away under the glare of florescent lights, our time on the beach becomes ever more a glowing and melancholy memory.

The sun, the surf, the gleaming sugar sand, the scent of coconut oil in the morning breeze, and the endless parade of women by the stand— all of them attainable—blend together into a great fuzzy meld in our recollection.

Every so often, listening to the car radio, a replay of one of the top-twenty hits of thirty summers ago will transport me back to a summer morning when the brine was thick in the air, the future was infinite, and anything was possible. To this day, whenever I hear *California Girls,* it's not just the memories of the summer of '65 that come flooding back, but the feelings—the emotions of a fleeting summer romance or the camaraderie of new found friends, both of them now long lost on the sea of years.

As with our memory of a dead loved one, so it is with our portrayal of happy, innocent times long past. It's human nature to be selectively romantic. It reminds me of John Steinbeck, who speaking through one of his characters, recalls the night he spent a good portion of his pay having a glass of champagne with a courtesan in her boudoir. He sweated and slaved away many endless days working in the sun and heat, but for the life of him, he could not recall in detail a single one of those days. But those few moments from this single night, he tells us, will stay forever in his memory with the clarity of a polished gem.

The One That Got Away

GORDON H. ('65-'73, '75) - Guarding on the beach, you meet many people from all walks of life. You meet families, rescue victims, lost children, guarding partners, and girlfriends. Most of the relationships are short-termed and relatively anonymous. Many, after an afternoon or a few days, leave your life forever. Then there are those people that stay with you—either as a memory or a lifelong friend.

There are many women I met on the beach whom today I could not even recall their last name if my life depended on it. But one stands out. Our acquaintance began one morning when I was setting up the beach, preparing for the day's work. When I went to tip over the lifeguard stand, someone had written something on the blackboard in the chalk we used to post water temperatures and tide tables. I don't even remember what the words were—a message to the effect, *"Can you guess who I am?"* This puzzled me for a few moments, and then it went out of my head as I began to deal with the crowd coming on the beach and the work ahead. The next morning, there was another message. Clearly, someone wanted my attention, but they were keeping their distance. During the slow moments of the day, I began to wonder who was messing with my head.

The next day was overcast and rainy. I spent the better part of the day under the surfboat with a book. When my partner woke up from his nap to go to lunch, a young girl sat down next to me and asked me about the book I was reading. It was probably something by Herman Hesse. She was exuberant and friendly and filled with curiosity. Very quickly, our conversation sped off, covering art, poetry, and places on the globe. It was a wild, free-association ramble of give and take chatter.

The conversation was so engrossing that I did not give much thought to her looks or her age. She was very attractive. She had short, dark, curly hair that framed bright eyes that exuded vitality. My interest took a new direction. When we got on to talking about her, I learned that she was about to enter her junior year in high school. She was sixteen. I was twenty-three. Too bad, I thought, she was well in advance of her years intellectually.

Later in the conversation, she revealed that it was she who had written on my blackboard. She had gotten the idea to correspond in chalk when she noticed the care I took with posting messages about the tides, temperatures, and little remarks and drawings I considered witty and posted for the benefit of anyone on the beach who cared to notice. At the time, I was studying architecture, so I took great care with my graphics.

From that day on, during the slow periods of the day, she would come by, and we would discuss the world and the interests we held. One day, our discussion fell upon the tides of phosphorous that sometimes came ashore. On those occasions, the waves or any water that is agitated glows. She found this impossible to believe and thought I was pulling her leg.

After I learned that she was renting a house just five or six houses down the street from my parent's place, I would walk up the beach in the evening and hope to run into her. On several occasions we did meet and talk into the evening.

Like all good things, it had to come to an end. Her family's vacation was over, and she would leave the following morning. Her family would go out to dinner that night after they had packed, and more than likely, we would never meet again.

That night I found myself missing her before she had left. Late in the evening, I walked by her family's rental. Her family had returned and was probably getting ready for bed. I wanted to talk to her one last time—to leave her with a special memory.

Hot dog! She was there. And she saw me walking by. She came over, and we walked over to the boardwalk and sat in the pavilion for a while. It was a perfect, mild, summer night, with the ocean at peace. Then, an idea hit me. Without telling her what I was doing, I took her by the hand and pulled her down to the water's edge. I started to dig in the sand. I'm sure she thought I was loopy, but I didn't care. I told her to get down on her hands and knees, and she squealed at what she finally saw: there, in the sand, were glowing traces of phosphorous. They gave off a tiny, greenish-blue glow when they were struck.

Had she been a little older, or myself a little younger, I would have picked her up and hugged and kissed her right there. But I didn't.

She left the next day. For a long time, we lost contact. Years later, when she called to tell me she was getting married, I was smitten.

We have continued to correspond ever since in a relationship that the rest of the world could barely understand. From her travels in Singapore and England, we have kept in touch. She is a reminder of the mystery of friendships. She is the phantom girl of Beach #6.

Watching The Water

MICKEY H. - After guarding for a couple of summers, you instinctively know what to look for while watching the water. You can tell when someone is in trouble or is about to get into trouble, usually before they do. You can see rips and other currents as if they were stained with some type of marker dye. It often amazes me how obvious these things are to me, while people all around me do not see them.

Watching the water has never left me. Whenever I go to the beach, I am always checking it out. I have made ocean rescues in Costa Rica, Mexico, and California just because I could see the problem developing and was able to get there in time. Sometimes, people standing near me have asked what I was doing as I started running toward the water to make a pull. In at least some of the cases, the person would probably have drowned if I had not been there because there were no lifeguards around and no one else who could swim good enough to get them in.

A Lifeguard's Epitaph

JACK C. - When there's a rescue, I want to be the one that's going. I didn't look around to see who was going.

♠ ♠ ♠

A Parting Wave

GORDON H. - In December 2004, toward the end of the research for this book, I got in touch with Rudy K., the oldest Lavallette lifeguard I had interviewed. I had last spoken with him on a Sunday afternoon six years previously. Tracking him down again was no easy task; he winters in Florida, and it took nearly twenty-five calls to find him. A widower, Rudy has also survived the loss of his two sons, Ralph and Roger. I'm sure it was difficult for him to talk about things that evoked their memory.

Finally, I reached Rudy on the phone, and we talked for an hour. The conversation was warm with reminisces; we talked about our shared past and mutual friends. He said it made him feel young again. Toward the end, I mentioned that one of the mysteries that I could not solve was the identity of the first female lifeguard in Lavallette. Some of the people I talked to said it was Janey Homer in '61 or '62. Another person maintained that it was a woman back in the '50s who had guarded briefly under unusual circumstances, but I could never get the details.

Almost as an afterthought to this puzzle, Rudy said, "You know about your mother, don't you?"

"I don't know what you mean," I replied.

He told me about events that occurred in the early 1950s—at the very margin of my life's memory—probably when I was five or six years old.

He explained that back then, the developed part of Lavallette was the north end of town. It was where the borough was first settled and was the "established" part of town. The north end had a boardwalk that ran half the town's length. People at the south end were considered "from the other side of the dunes." Services to them were minimal and perfunctory.

At the end of the summer, the Lavallette Beach Patrol was reduced to a skeleton crew. The beaches at the north end got lifeguards, but the south did not. My mother spoke to town officials to express her concern that the people of the south end were not getting the same services for their taxes.

The officials turned a deaf ear to her concerns. They replied that there were more people in the north end, and the south end was sparsely populated. I can vaguely remember they told her—the mother of three small children—that she was expected to walk or drive a half-mile to go to protected beaches rather than go to the beach at the end of her street.

I knew my mother, the former Carol MacKinnon, before she married my father, Louis Hesse, was certified as a Red Cross water safety instructor and had worked with the disabled in aquatic programs. But I don't recall her ever telling me she had worked as a lifeguard. She was a willful woman with a strong sense of fairness and justice. Considering the alternatives and the inequity of the situation, she took her old lake and pool rescue equipment to the beach and became a volunteer lifeguard on the ocean for her own children as well as the neighbors.

The officials reconsidered (or were shamed into taking some kind of face-saving action). They ended up placing borough lifesaving equipment at her disposal. As a child, I knew she had challenged the officials, and there was some resentment of her making waves, but I did not recall the outcome.

Rudy's comments placed these events from long ago into context, fitting pieces of a puzzle in place so that I could see the picture. It came to me as a revelation.

In essence, although unpaid, my mother became the "first" female lifeguard sanctioned by the town. This was a question I had not been able to nail down in countless discussions over the years. That the answer should come to me in such a roundabout way, and be so personal, stirred a part of me that had not been touched since she died.

My mother was instrumental in my learning to swim. She waited patiently on Saturdays while I took swimming lessons at the Westfield, New Jersey YMCA. (She is part of the reason I feel such a strong affinity for the "Y," and it is where I work today.) She helped pull me from the water when I was six and a struggling swimmer; she would spend hours on the beach looking for me while most of the time I was underwater looking for "treasures." She was there almost every time I wanted to show her some aquatic feat—and those countless times when I would say, "Look at me!" She was gently righteous and tried to do good where she could. By her example, I learned respect for the act of mothering and for the ocean.

As I contemplated this revelation from Rudy, it was as if from somewhere in the hereafter, I could almost see her, the ocean at her back and the salty breeze in her hair, smiling. In a way, this discovery was, from her, a parting wave.

The former Carol MacKinnon stands proudly wearing her lifeguard suit with its Red Cross insignia (circa 1940). She was, most likely, the first female lifeguard on the ocean in Lavallette.

Two female guards head out through the surf in a Hankins. Once only the domain of male lifeguards, women now routinely workout in the surfboats and compete in tournaments.

Epilogue

The following are brief descriptions of the subsequent lives of some of the people quoted and mentioned in this book.

In a few cases, when an individual could not be located or contacted, limited third party information was gathered, and the person's actual name was not used.

In three cases, characters were created that are composites of various people. This was done at the request of individuals who wanted to remain annonymous in the events described and by the author to protect the innocent.

The years shown are the years they patrolled the beach.

Quoted in the text:

Andy B. - Andy Baran ('65-'70)

After leaving lifeguarding, Andy graduated from Monmouth College in New Jersey, and in 1973, became a probation officer in the Ocean County Probation Department. He married, earned a masters degree, had two daughters by his first marriage, divorced, remarried, and moved to Toms River, New Jersey. He was named Supervisor of the Year in 1989 by the Probation Association of New Jersey. After several promotions, he retired as a Principal Probation Officer, and in early 2000, moved to northern New York state. It was there, on June 2, 2002—the day before his fifty-fifth birthday—that he died of an apparent massive heart attack. A Lavallette Beach Patrol surfboat has been dedicated in his memory, and a scholarship fund has been established in his name by the probation department for which he served nearly thirty years. One of his colleagues said of him, "Andy was the greatest mentor I will ever know, and I try to live up to his example every day of my life."

Archie M. - Archie Mrozek ('58-'64)

Archie, or Art, as he is sometimes known, is vice president of a precious metals company and resides in Lavallette, New Jersey. He also sells real estate.

Bob G. - Bob Ginglen ('63-'67, '69)

Bob attended the University of Richmond in Virginia and earned a degree in history. His brother, Dick, served as captain of the Lavallette Beach Patrol in the mid-1960s. After lifeguarding, Bob entered the paper products business. He and his wife, the former Caroline Bogdewic, live in Lavallette, New Jersey.

Bobbi A. - Barbara "Bobbi" Alesso DeMuro ('65-'69)

Bobbi became an elementary school teacher, married, and is the mother of Jeff, who guarded for the Lavallette Beach Patrol, and daughter Jayme, who worked for the beach police. She now lives in Lavallette, New Jersey all year long with her husband Pete. Although they consider golf their "major job," they continue to love going to the beach in the summer.

Butch S. - Butch Spicoli (a composite character) (mid-'60s)

Butch went on to become a well-known member of his community. He spends much of his leisure time fishing.

Charlie B. - Charles Badeau ('65, '67-'71)

Charlie was last seen in Point Pleasant Beach, New Jersey in the late 1990s. His current whereabouts are unknown.

Dave M. - Dave McConnell (late '60s, '74)

Dave attended the University of Miami on a swimming scholarship and lifeguarded his junior and senior years in Florida. He earned degrees in physical education, science, and math and became an insurance salesman for Prudential for twenty-eight years before retiring in 2001. Dave and his wife, the former Sharon Limburg, raised two sons, now twenty-two and twenty-four years old. Now that his sons are out of college, Dave hopes to buy a boat and sail the islands of the Bahamas.

Dick H. - Dick Hoffman ('50-2000; Captain '66-'80)

Dick continued to work at the Jersey Shore until 2000. He taught industrial arts for thirty-four years before retiring. He had one son by his first marriage, divorced, and married Sue Johnson, a prominent local elected official. The two alternate their time between living in Lavallette and in Florida at Fort Meyers and Boca Raton and enjoy traveling together.

Edwardo B. – Edwardo Black ('69-'70)

Whereabouts unknown.

Gordon H. - Gordon Hesse ('65-'73, '75)

Gordon became a probation officer with the Ocean County, New Jersey Probation Department. He served as an investigator, and later as the coordinator of a Big Brothers-type volunteer program before embarking on a public relations and public affairs career, most notably for Kimball Medical Center in Lakewood, New Jersey; Lincoln University in Pennsylvania; the New Castle County Department of Libraries in Delaware; the University of Delaware; and the YMCA of Delaware in Wilmington. He married, had one son, Conor, and was recently divorced. He lives in Ardencroft, Delaware.

Hobie - Cedric Huff (a composite character) ('65-'74)

Hobie went to work for non-profit organizations and continues to center much of his activities on the ocean.

Jack C. - Jack Caucino ('77-present)

Jack attended St. John's University in New York on a swimming scholarship (distance freestyle and butterfly events) and graduated with a degree in business administration. He comes from a family of life-guards, each of whom have gained recognition as top competitors in lifeguard tournaments. His brothers and sister all guarded: Carl, from '71 to '75; Joe from '76 to present; and Julie from '77 to '81. Jack has won several Ironman competitions. With his brother, Joe, he won regional rowing events three years in a row, and they placed in the top ten in national competitions several times. He continues to compete in tournaments. In 1996, while coaching at Ocean County College in Toms River, New Jersey, he was named National Coach of the Year. He is the director of aquatics at the Community YMCA of Red Bank, New Jersey, and a teacher. For the last eight years, he has coached swimming at the "Y" with teams that, he notes, have reached national prominence. His wife, the former Pam Okolita, works as a beach badge checker. They live in Howell, New Jersey.

Jim C. - Jim Cresbaugh ('67-present; Captain '81-present)

Jim graduated with a bachelor's degree in physical education and went on to earn a master's degree in educational administration from Temple University in Philadelphia, Pennsylvania. He became the manager and lifeguard captain of the Lavallette Beach Patrol in 1981 and continues to serve in that capacity during the summer. He is an assistant principal at Mountain Lakes High School in New Jersey. His wife, the former Lori Bailey, and daughters, Jamie, Keri and Casey, live with him in Sparta, New Jersey in the off season. Daughter Jamie has worked as a lifeguard on the Barnegat Bay beaches in Lavallette, making it three generations of Cresbaughs who have worked at the beach simultaneously. (His mother has served as a dispatcher for ten years.) As captain of the guards, Jim has developed professional U.S. Lifesaving Association standards for the men and women he supervises. They have won numerous lifeguarding competitions. Jim was named an All-Century Lifeguard by the *Asbury Park Press* in 2000 along with other Lavallette Beach Patrol veterans Rudy Krone and Joe Caucino.

Jim Sim - Jim Simms ('63-'77)

Jim lifeguarded in Monmouth County, New Jersey and was heavily involved in lifeguard tournaments for years. He became a school principal. Attempts to reach him were unsuccessful.

Jimmy A. - Jim Alesso ('66-'67)

After attending Fairleigh Dickenson College in Teaneck, New Jersey, Jim completed studies at the American Academy McAllister Institute of Funeral Service, Inc. in Manhattan. In 1972, he became director of Alesso's Funeral Home in Lodi, New Jersey, which was established by his father in 1949. He has two grown children, Peter and Lauren. Jim is an avid hunter.

Joe S. - Joe Silvestri ('68-'76, '90s, '00s)

After graduating from Strayer University in Washington, D.C. with a degree in public administration, Joe went on to become an administrator for several area hospitals. He is married to the former Sharon McCloskey with one son, Joseph "J.J." Silvestri, Jr., and lives in Toms River, New Jersey. He has continued to be "on call" for the Lavallette Beach Patrol and has served there intermittently during the past two decades.

John M. - John Marra ('46-'53; Captain '52-'53)

John was a leading scorer for Orange High School when they won the New Jersey High School Basketball Tournament. He is the all-time leading basketball scorer for Panzer College (later incorporated into Montclair State University in New Jersey). Later, he refereed college games. His daughter also became a referee and became the first female inducted into the men's basketball association. John is well known in the paper products business, having been in that industry for more than fifty years, serving as the vice president of a company that produces boxes and other paper products. While a lifeguard, he met his wife-to-be, Dione Campomensosi of Fort Lee, New Jersey, on the Fourth of July on the beach at Washington Avenue in Lavallette. They have three children, John Jr., Cindy, and Jeffrey, five grandchildren, and two great grandchildren.

John V. - John Van Dorpe ('66-'70)

John graduated from the Newark College of Engineering in New Jersey with a degree in mechanical engineering in 1970. He met the former Marguerite Tacketto on the beach at New York Avenue in Lavallette in 1968, and they were wed six years later. Their daughter, Tracy, has multiple degrees from Dartmouth College in New Hampshire and is the assistant director of the HBS Fund at Harvard Business School in Massachusetts. John opened his own engineering business in 1985 and merged with Maser Consulting in Middletown, New Jersey in 1990. He is vice president and director of utility engineering. John and Marguerite live on Barnegat Bay in Toms River, New Jersey and also maintain a residence in Lavallette.

Jon S. - Jon Slayback ('66-'74)

Jon attended and graduated from Syracuse University in New York with a degree in geography. He taught for two years in the early 1970s and then moved to North Creek, New York to ski at Gore Mountain. He began and continues to operate Slayback Construction. He recently married the former Julie Smith.

Kenny A. - Kenny Andersch (surfer) ('60s-'90s)

Ken, better known as "Paddlefoot" among the surfers of the shore area, founded Nicoya's Jack of Arts in 1976, dealing in South American arts and crafts. In 1984, he bought Ortley Stone and Gravel and started Ortley Garden Center and Andersch's Landscaping and Design. His business has grown, and he has become a strong presence in world-wide internet marketing services. He has one son, A.J., and continues to live in Ortley Beach, New Jersey, the west coast of Florida, and the Florida Keys.

Kenny J. - Ken Jones ('67-'69)

Ken Jones graduated with a degree in industrial education from Clemson University in South Carolina and masters level studies in photography at the University of Florida. His career has taken him from being a southwest river rafting guide, to a software tech support expert, to flying in helicopters taking photos over Hawaii, to selling cars in Los Angeles, to directing the graduate studies program at Peace Theological Seminary (PTS) in Los Angeles, to currently working with a major financial services company. Ken lives with his wife, Carol, at PTS where they are enrolled in the Doctor of Spiritual Science program. His major playtime interests are wilderness survival and enjoyment.

Michelle P. - Michelle Pierce ('77-'80, '83-'84)

Michelle began swimming competitively when she was ten years old and lifeguarded at pools and swim clubs before working on the ocean. She received a B.S. in nutrition from Penn State in 1980 and her M.S. in the same field from the University of Delaware in 1985. She worked in the Migrant Farm Workers Program in Colorado before earning her Ph.D. at the University of Connecticut in 1998. She is currently an assistant extension professor in residence at U.C. Her interests include childhood obesity, anemia, food security, and sustainable agriculture. Michelle has "three great kids," and they enjoy water skiing together. She is very proud of her organic garden.

Mickey H. - Mickey Howes ('67-'76)

Mickey graduated from San Diego State University in California with a degree in geography. He traveled extensively after college, visiting South and Central America, often surfing unexplored surfing breaks. In California, he was a city planner for Escondido and Carlsbad over ten years before becoming a planning consultant for Hofman Planning Associates fifteen years ago. He wed the former Christy Lubberstedt twenty years ago, and they have one son, Dylan. The family has traveled to Hawaii on several occasions. His office is located ten minutes from the Pacific, and he occasionally goes surfing during lunch breaks. He still frequents remote coastal sections of Mexico as the opportunity arises. "One summer in New Jersey is three times as intense as in California: on the East Coast there is only a limited time for people to throw off their clothes and get into the ocean," Mickey said. "Here it is all year long so there is little sense of time and opportunity fleeting."

Mike H. - Gordon "Mike" Howes ('39-'41, '46-'54)

Mike flew B-24s on photoreconnaissance missions over China, Burma, and the Philippines during World War II. After the war, he worked for the American Red Cross for fifty years. As director of water safety, he taught thousands of kids to swim. After retiring in 1982, he became a first mate and purser on the sailing vessel *St. Christopher.* In the 1990s, he was inducted into the East Coast Surfing Legends Hall of Fame. His son, Mickey, and daughter, Colleen, went on to become life-guards. Mike now lives in Bradenton, Florida.

Patricia D. - Pat Dughi ('67-'69)

Patty is an elementary school teacher living in Mapleshade, New Jersey with her husband and teenage son.

Paul T. - Paul Tilton ('66-'73)

Paul earned a degree in civil engineering from the New Jersey Institute of Technology (NJIT) and taught for eight years before going into homebuilding full time. He now has his own construction company, T and H Homes Incorporated, and lives on the bay in the Silverton section of Toms River, New Jersey with his wife, the former JoAnn Shutaris, and his young daughter, Kira.

Randy S. - Randy Smith (a composite character) ('60s)

Randy graduated from college and went into his family's business. He suffered several financial reversals and died in his early forties. Some say his death was the consequence of too many risky excesses. He never married.

Ray B. - Ray Birchler ('55-'60)

After graduating from Villanova University in Pennsylvania with a degree in economics, Ray established Raymond A. Birchler Realtors in Lavallette in 1965. He is now partially retired and lives in Lavallette. He qualified as a real estate expert before the Superior Court of New Jersey and also serves as tax commissioner of Ocean County and con-demnation commissioner as appointed by the Superior Court of New

Jersey. His son, Eric, now handles day-to-day operations of the business his father founded; his other son, Ray, Jr., is a GIS specialist with a Ph.D. in computers. Ray continued his lifesaving work, serving seventeen years on the Lavallette First Aid Squad.

Rudy K. - Rudy Krone ('32-mid-'40s; Captain)

Following WWII, Rudy operated Krone's Tavern in Lavallette. His business thrived and grew to include two more bars and restaurants. Until recently, he was an avid hunter and skier, skiing major courses in the U.S. and Europe. He spends his summers in Lavallette and winters in Lake Worth, Florida.

Russell F. - Russell Frazier ('50-'51)

Russell graduated from Brown University in Rhode Island with a liberal arts degree and served in the U.S. Navy from 1957 to 1959, becoming a lieutenant, junior grade. He later worked for Regal Paper in New Jersey for several years before starting Frazier Packaging Corp. He sold this business five years later to Coca Cola, and worked for their food division for ten years. He started his own business again in coffee, tea, and extracts, which he continues to operate under the Frazier Packaging name. He lives in Lavallette and Pompano Beach, Florida. His wife is the former Marge Phillips, and they have three grown children, Russell, Jeannie, and Susan.

Sam H. - Sam Hammer ('62-'68)

Sam, along with his wife, the former Louise Coxson, is the owner and operator of the Crab's Claw Inn, a well-known Lavallette bar and restaurant. A graduate of West Virginia University, he attends every WVU football game he can. They have two grown children, Shannon, a French teacher, and Sammy IV, a professional surfer. In the off-season, they vacation at Islamorada in the Flordia Keys.

Sharon M. - Sharon Mill (beachgoer) ('60s-present)

Sharon graduated from Ohio University with a degree in speech therapy, married a lifeguard, raised a daughter, and was recently divorced. In a teaching career that has spanned thirty years, she has most recently been teaching autistic children. She continues to visit Lavallette in the summer and looks forward to learning Italian and reading when she retires.

Tom A. - Tom Azzolini ('63-'70)

Tom attended Jersey City State College, earning a degree in education. He went on to earn masters degrees in reading education and administration and supervision. He retired as the principal of Toms River High School South in 2000. He and his wife, the former Arlene Rossi, have two grown children, Jennifer and Tom, and live in the Silver Bay section of Toms River, New Jersey. Tom describes retirement as "man's greatest invention" and spends part of his leisure time on a twenty-two-foot Mako fishing boat.

Mentioned in the text:

Bill Kemble ('50s-'70s)

Bill remained a beloved fixture in the Lavallette Beach Patrol Headquarters for more than thirty years before his death in the mid-1970s. His helpful, calm, assuring manner and playfulness were appreciated by all the senior guards and most of the rookies. A Lavallette Lifeguard Tournament is named in his honor.

Charles Hankins

The Hankins boatworks was started by Charles Hankins' father in 1912 and is estimated to have produced nine thousand boats. Charles Hankins closed his shop for full-time boat building in the early 1990s and died in June 2003. His shop in Lavallette became a museum in October 2004. The boats built by his family continue to be venerated. A classic Hankins New Jersey sea skiff was built in 1993 for a special display on the National Mall in Washington, D.C. when he was honored by the National Endowment for the Arts. A 1991 New Jersey Network documentary, *The Sea Bright Skiff: Working on the Jersey Shore,* featured boats built by the Hankins family.

"Duke" - Frank DeLuca ('60s)

A colorful lifeguard, "Duke" was last known to have been living in the Orlando, Florida area, where he ran a car dealership. He has not been heard from since.

Eddie V. - Eddie Verna (early '60s)

Ed could not be contacted before publication. He continues to live in Lavallette, New Jersey.

"Jake" J. - Tom Jacobsen ('65-'69)

Died of self-inflicted gunshot wound.

Pete Locascio ('64-'74)

Pete graduated from New Jersey's Rutgers University in 1964 and Seton Hall Law School in 1972. He wed the former Pat DiMartino, and they have been "married for 127 years." Peter has become a successful attorney and municipal judge. He lives wherever he goes and resides in Atlantic Highlands, New Jersey. Their daughter, Gianna, is working toward her Doctorate in Psychology at Rutgers, and their son, Peter, recently graduated from Rowan University in New Jersey.

Roger K. - Roger Krone ('64-'68)

Died of a gunshot wound.

John T. - John Tawgin ('64-'65, '69)

John graduated with an MBA from the University of Massachusetts and worked in New York for an advertising agency. In 1972, he started his own business, John Shawn Productions. His photo concession business, seen in many theme parks, now employs more than five hundred people servicing such accounts as Sea World, Universal, Great Adventure, and Radio City Music Hall. His company was voted one of the best to work for in New Jersey. He has been featured in the career section of Forbes Magazine. He resides in Mantoloking, New Jersey and Aspen, Colorado.

"The Whale" – Dominic Arena (late '50s)

Dominic's whereabouts are unknown.

The rescue board is one of the fastest ways to reach a victim. Typically eleven or twelve feet long, they can support a number of people and are ideal for patrolling a swimming area. This photo was taken during a lifeguard tournament in 1980.

Glossary

Gear, Surf Conditions, & Jargon

GEAR

Acme Thunderer Metal whistles favored by lifeguards before the advent of Fox whistles.

Bench The lifeguard stand. In recent years, the stands in Lavallette have increased in height to where the seat is above the eye level of someone standing next to it.

Can A term that refers to earlier metal forms of the torpedo buoy.

Gunwale or Gunnel The upper edge of a boat or a ship. The oarlocks are mounted on the gunnels.

Line Rope attached to torpedo buoys and used to pull victims and lifeguards to shore. In all too many accounts, overzealous beachgoers have tried to "help" guards by pulling in the line—often before the guards were ready, or pulling too fast, dragging the rescuers underwater.

Line box Line (to attach to the torpedo buoy when a rescue would involve extremely strong currents or many victims) was sometimes stored on reels, which were later replaced by boxes. The line was usually about one thousand feet long.

Gear, continued

Neat's-foot oil   An oil used to protect leather that is exposed to moisture and saltwater.

Oarlocks   Fixtures to provide a fulcrum for rowing oars. They may be constructed of wooden pins, swivel fittings, or fixed, curved brass designs.

Red flags   Flags posted near the beach to indicate surf conditions are unsafe for swimming.

Rescue belts   Cloth and/or leather belts with a large metal loop to attach torpedo buoy clips. They are worn loosely over the guards' swimsuits. They were introduced to reduce the cutting action of the older loops, which were worn over the shoulder. (The looped harnesses have come back into popular usage in recent years.) By raising the belt above the waist during a rescue where a line is used, it helps to insure that the guard and victim are not pulled under water.

Sausage   Refers to foam rubber torpedo buoys, so named because they were soft and bended easily to form a belt around a victim.

Surfboat   A boat designed to go through large breaking waves. Adapted from the Sea Bright Skiff, perhaps the best known is the Hankins surfboat. Weighing more than three hundred pounds and stretching about seventeen feet, the Hankins boats have been made since the Depression Days. Van Dyne and Robinson fiberglass boats have begun to replace the Hankins boats.

Torpedo buoy   A flotation device approximately nine inches in diameter and three feet long with grips for victims to hold onto. Originally, they were hollow and made of metal with rope running longitudinally. Eventually, they were constructed of either cork, polystyrene, foam rubber, or high impact plastic. In the early days, the rope created a large loop to fit over the head and shoulder of the lifeguard. Eventually, at some beaches, a clip replaced this rope loop, and guards wore leather and canvas belts with large brass rings to receive the clip.

SURF CONDITIONS

Close-out   Refers to waves that break their entire length at one moment.

Comber   A large wave that rolls or breaks on a beach or sandbar.

Jetties   Long piles of rocks and/or bulkheads extending into the ocean, designed to slow down strong, beach-eroding currents. Lavallette's jetties were designed to be covered by high tides.

Rip   See *Rip Current.*

Rip Current   A current going away from shore and out to sea, sometimes as far as several hundred feet. It is often referred to as a rip, a run, a seapuss, an undertow, or (erroneously) a riptide. (The U.S. Lifeguard Association is recommending the use of the term "rip current" to avoid confusion with these other names for the same phenomena.) The rip current is created when sets of waves deposit large volumes of water over a sandbar. In seeking its own level, the current moves to the deepest water and "drains" out to sea. During or after a storm at sea, rip currents tend to be most dangerous, pulling unwary swimmers away from the shoreline. They often panic when they find the current too strong and tire quickly. The best way to deal with getting caught in a rip current is to swim to the side; they are usually no more than twenty feet wide.

Run   See *Rip Current.*

Sandbar   A narrow shoal formed along the shore by the sand-depositing action of the currents or tides. Sandbars can change rapidly or remain the same for weeks at a time. The shape and shallowness of the sandbar determines where waves will break and the drainage of the waves. See *Rip Current.*

Seapuss   A term of unknown origin, but used extensively along the Jersey Shore. See *Rip Current.*

Set   A group of waves in a series interspersed with periods of relative calm.

Shorebreak   A condition where high tide wave energy terminates sharply on the beach, often knocking over bathers who have miscalculated their location or the force of the wave. The brutality of shorebreaks increases as the slope of the beach into the water increases, and the expended waves drain with their own force.

Surf Conditions, continued

Shoulder
The part of the wave that is about to fold over. This is the most desirable part of the wave to ride when body surfing, boogie boarding, and surfboating.

Undertow
See *Rip Current.*

Wash
The place on the shoreline between where the waves break and reach before draining back into the ocean.

JARGON

Broaching
To roll a boat. This usually refers to a surfboat with its longitudinal axis parallel to the oncoming wave. This presents a hazard not only to the occupants of the boat, but also to anyone in the path of the formerly inanimate object that has abruptly acquired the attributes of a locomotive.

Double ball hangout
Also known as a DBL. This involves an intricate maneuver wherein the ventilation properties of the bathing suit are increased for maximum anatomical exposure to air and sunlight.

Double Eagle
The difficult and stunning tandem acrobatic created when two people agree to lock arms back-to-back and "moon" simultaneously while one bends over, swinging his partner in a half tuck on his back. There are no documented cases of this maneuver ever being performed successfully when either party was sober; however, there are numerous cases reported where it failed because the parties were not sober.

Double screamer
A lifeguard whistle of high attention-grabbing magnitude. When properly used, it garners the attention of almost everyone on the beach; when used too frequently or abused, it causes thoughts of lifeguard homicide by people trying to savor the tranquility of their vacation.

Dropping in
The point at which a surf rider comes down the face of the wave. Depending upon circumstances, this may be a moment of great thrill or absolute terror.

Hand jobs
Rescues that involve more running than swimming, hence not requiring a torpedo buoy. In many case, these involve helping small children or the aging when they have fallen down in the wash.

Jerk ball	Attributed to Pete L., in a fit of pique, when in search of a previously unknown—and therefore socially acceptable—derogatory expression.
Mooning	Lowering one's head toward the knees while exposing the exterior of the resulting crease.
Party boats	Boats with large decks around their entire perimeter for sport fishermen. Also known as day boats or head boats.
Pearling	Originally, this referred to the shiny, "pearl-like" bubble that is formed over the nose or bow of a surfboard on a wave as it begins to go below the surface of the water, usually ejecting its rider aloft. It can also refer to a surfboat that comes down a large wave at too steep an angle, driving its bow underwater.
Pebbles	A juvenile and masochistic game created by guards gone stir crazy on a slow day with a shorebreak. The object is to lie in the wash and let waves move the inert human form at their whim.
Pressed ham	"Mooning" against a piece of glass, usually a window of a car or van.
Pull	A rescue.
Snapper	A baby bluefish; also sometimes used as slang referring to young ladies who hung around lifeguard stands "trolling" for the attention of the guards, occasionally distracting them from their duties. Synonymous with Split Tails.
Time investment	Also known as a T.I. Refers to inordinate amounts of attention given to young ladies before they have reached the age of legal consent in the hopes of accumulating chips that may one day be cashed in for bonus prizes.

Built for a crew of one, two, or three lifeguards, Hankins surfboats were at times used for frolicking, as seen in this photo from the early 1950s.

Acknowledgments

The following people have been extremely helpful in compiling this undertaking. I would like to thank them for their contributions.

For sharing their experience—Sam Hammer, Joe Silvestri, Pat Dughi, Barbara "Bobbi" Alesso DeMuro, Jim Alesso, John Van Dorpe, Sharon Mill, Jon Slayback, Paul Tilton, Charles Ballou, Ken Jones, Bob Ginglen, Jack Caucino, Dave McConnell, Dick Hoffman, Kenny Andersch, Michelle Bitzer Pierce, Ray Birchler, Archie Mrozek, Tom Azzolini, Bob Tormollan, and Mickey, Colleen, and Mike Howes.

Special thanks to Jim Cresbaugh and Rudy Krone.

For the chills, spills, and thrills and other indescribable memories—Charles Hankins.

For encouragement and inspiration—John Tawgin, John Marra, Russell Frazier, Brenda Lange, Judy Baker, Jim Clerico, Ted Caddell, Sara Kehew, and The Phantom Girl on Beach #6, Carol.

For gracious hosting—John Tawgin, Diane Ault, Paul Cullen, and Herb Jones and his family.

For patience, forbearance, and latitude—Louis Conor Kanon Hesse, my son, and Melanie Ryan Hesse, my former wife.

I would also like to acknowledge George Valente, my editor, for his contribution to this work; his patience, meticulous editing, and attention to detail helped organize wandering ideas.

If you have an experience or anecdote about lifeguarding, please send your comments to: Gordon Hesse c/o Jersey Shore Publications, P.O. Box 176, Bay Head, NJ 08742; or go to www.gordonhesse.com.

A portion of the proceeds from this book will be donated to the Lavallette Lifeguard Alumni Association.

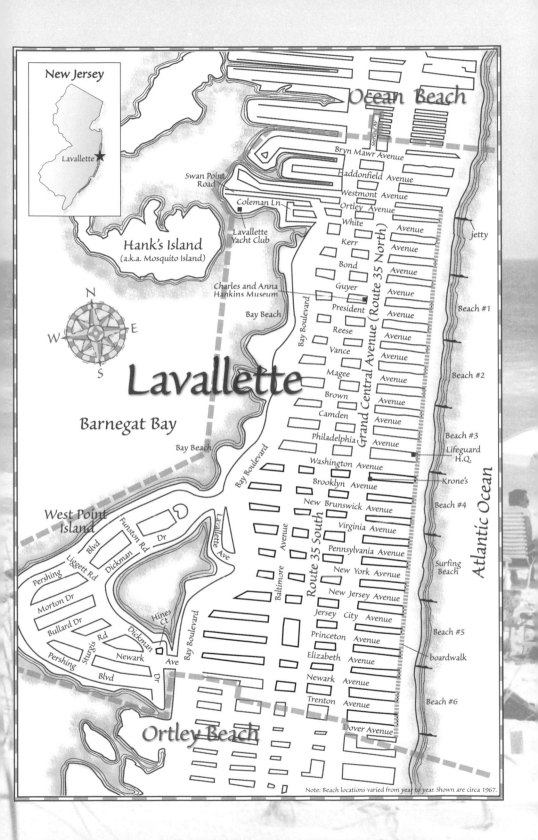

Lavallette

New Jersey
Lavallette

Ocean Beach

Sterling Av
Bryn Mawr Avenue
Haddonfield Avenue
Westmont Avenue
Ortley Avenue
White   Avenue
Kerr   Avenue
Bond   Avenue
Guyer   Avenue
President   Avenue
Reese   Avenue
Vance   Avenue
Magee   Avenue
Brown   Avenue
Camden   Avenue
Philadelphia   Avenue
Washington Avenue
Brooklyn   Avenue
New Brunswick Avenue
Virginia Avenue
Pennsylvania Avenue
New York Avenue
New Jersey Avenue
Jersey   City   Avenue
Princeton   Avenue
Elizabeth   Avenue
Newark   Avenue
Trenton   Avenue
Dover Avenue

Grand Central Avenue (Route 35 North)
Route 35 South

Bay Boulevard
Bay Boulevard
Bay Boulevard

Swan Point Road
Coleman Ln
Lavallette Yacht Club
Charles and Anna Hankins Museum
Bay Beach
Bay Beach

Hank's Island
(a.k.a. Mosquito Island)

Barnegat Bay

West Point Island

Funston Rd
Lavallette Ave
Dr
Blvd
Liggett Rd
Pershing
Dickman
Morton Dr
Bullard Dr
Sturgis Rd
Dickman
Hines Ct
Newark
Pershing   Blvd
Dr
Bay Boulevard
Ave
Baltimore   Avenue

N
W   E
S

jetty
Beach #1
Beach #2
Beach #3
Lifeguard H.Q.
Krone's
Beach #4
Surfing Beach
Beach #5
boardwalk
Beach #6

Atlantic Ocean

Ortley Beach

Note: Beach locations varied from year to year. Shown are circa 1967.